AQUASH'S MURDER

Hermeneutical and Post-Modern Legal Analysis in Light of the Murder of Anna Mae Pictou-Aquash

GREGG WAGER

Aquash's Murder: Hermeneutical and Post-Modern Legal Analysis in Light of the Murder of Anna Mae Pictou-Aquash
Copyright © 2023/2024 Gregg Wager

Published by:
Trine Day LLC
PO Box 577
Walterville, OR 97489
1-800-556-2012
www.TrineDay.com
TrineDay@icloud.com

Library of Congress Control Number: 2023952278

Wager, Gregg.
–1st ed.
p. cm.

Epub (ISBN-13) 978-1-63424-451-0
Trade Paperback (ISBN-13) 978-1-63424-450-3
1. Aquash, Anna Mae, 1945-1976. 2. Hermeneutics. 3. Responsibility Philosophy. 4. Indians of North America Government relation. 5. United States. Federal Bureau of Investigation. 6. American Indian Movement History 7. Peltier, Leonard, (1944- ...) I. Wager, Gregg. II. Title

First Edition
10 9 8 7 6 5 4 3 2 1

Printed in the USA
Distribution to the Trade by:
Independent Publishers Group (IPG)
814 North Franklin Street
Chicago, Illinois 60610
312.337.0747
www.ipgbook.com

Be not afeard. The isle is full of noises,
Sounds and sweet airs that give delight and hurt not.
Sometimes a thousand twangling instruments
Will hum about mine ears, and sometimes voices
That, if I then had waked after long sleep,
Will make me sleep again; and then, in dreaming,
The clouds methought would open, and show riches
Ready to drop upon me, that when I waked
I cried to dream again.
– Caliban, *The Tempest*: Act 3, Scene 2
William Shakespeare

CONTENTS

FOREWORD

By Barry Bachrach

In July of 2011, at a symposium sponsored by the Native American Journalists Association, I spoke about the murder investigation into the December 1975 execution of Anna Mae Aquash and its connection with events surrounding the imprisonment of Leonard Peltier for the alleged execution of two FBI agents in June of 1975. I began critically researching her murder in 2004 shortly after a jury found Arlo Looking Cloud, a young AIM member, guilty of being an accessory to her murder. Though nearly thirty years had passed since her body was found, Looking Cloud was the first person tried for her murder.

I was representing Leonard Peltier at that time, and I realized what occurred during Looking Cloud's trial posed a great challenge to the release of Peltier who was then due for a parole hearing in 2008. Immediately following Looking Cloud's trial, I expressed that realization in a statement released to the press: "The trial was well-orchestrated – not to convict the man on trial, but to convict AIM activists and prosecute Leonard Peltier all over again (another violation of his Constitutional Rights, I would argue) in the court of public opinion." In the aftermath of the trial, I also became aware of various media containing shadowy allegations about Peltier giving the order to have Anna Mae killed; allegations never made at trial. This was reported in papers and internet commentary.

I firmly believed that Peltier had nothing to do with her murder, and, therefore, decided that his representation compelled me to conduct a thorough investigation into Ms. Aquash's murder to expose the shadowy allegations as lies. I have no evidence that Peltier was involved in planning the murder of, giving the order to murder, or committing the murder of Ms. Aquash. To this day, I have continued my research in connection with representing Arlo Looking Cloud commencing in February 2008 and then in relation with several projects in which I was involved. As a result, I discovered many peculiar twists and turns in this case and the troubling manner in which it has been investigated and misused by the FBI.

Today, despite a few answers as to what actually occurred, the case continues to spawn many new questions as we continue to seek truth. As Dr. Wager posits in his book, "This study cannot exhaustively examine all dilemmas of the Anna Mae Pictou-Aquash case, let alone conclusively solve any of them." Neither will I attempt to do so here. I do, however, want to touch on some key points which are more fully elucidated in Dr. Wager's work.

I have long believed that the reason the FBI did not immediately solve the murder arose because informants or operatives were involved in Ms. Aquash's murder, similar to the Whitey Bulger episode in Boston. Were government informants or operatives closely involved in her murder? If not, why did it take the government nearly 30 years to indict and convict Looking Cloud, especially when FBI documents reveal that the FBI knew the names of the three alleged culprits within weeks of her murder?

To date, I cannot answer those questions without simply offering my belief as to the identity of involved informants and/or operatives. Belief, however, is not fact. That said, it is beyond question that the FBI took very dubious actions in the investigation of this murder from its inception. Within months of her body being found, an article in the July 1976 edition of **Content**, Canada's national news media magazine, questioned the on and off news coverage of Anna Mae's murder, especially when a U.S. Civil Rights Commission had already concluded, "[T]here is sufficient credibility in reports reaching this office to cast doubt on the propriety of actions by the FBI, and to raise questions about their impartiality and focus." The author of the article, Barrie Zwicker, wrote: "She was murdered under mysterious circumstances … The FBI was deeply involved. Many close to the case charge that the FBI murdered Mrs. Aquash."

Did the government initially fail or refuse to prosecute Aquash's murder because of the specter that the FBI was involved? Put otherwise, did the government determine that the risk of conducting a meaningful investigation into Aquash's murder posed too great a risk of exposing FBI wrongdoing? If so, what changed over the course of the next 27 years that resulted in Looking Cloud's indictment?

While the government continued some limited investigation, the general public was kept in the dark. Putting aside that the FBI knew within weeks of the murder who was directly involved, and Arlo Looking Cloud had provided information in 1995, that he and Theda Nelson Clarke were present when Aquash was executed at point blank range by John Graham, the government refused or failed to take any action. It was Russell Means, a Colorado AIM leader, who publicly denounced AIM on November 3, 1999, when he, Robert Pictou Branscombe, and Ward Churchill, conducted a news conference. Means, a former AIM leader, accused Vernon Bellecourt, head of security for AIM, of giving orders to his brother Clyde to have Aquash executed. Means named Arlo Looking Cloud, John Graham, and Theda Nelson Clarke as the persons who carried out the order.

In 1999, Peltier was mounting a strong clemency campaign in the waning years of the Clinton administration. Peltier did not receive clemency from President Clinton and the government did not then prosecute anyone for the murder of Ms. Aquash. But, off the momentum of his initial failed clemency campaign, Peltier continued to pursue avenues for release. Arlo Looking Cloud was indicted in March of 2003, and arrested on March 27, 2003, for the murder of Anna Mae Aquash.

In November 2003, the United States Circuit Court of Appeals for the Tenth Circuit rejected Peltier's appeal of the parole commission's denial of parole and set his next hearing for 2008. However, in doing so, the Tenth Circuit acknowledged: **"Much of the government's behavior at the Pine Ridge reservation and in its prosecution of Peltier is to be condemned. The government withheld evidence. It intimidated witnesses. These facts are not disputed."** Yet, the court ruled that it lacked power to overturn the parole commission's decision under applicable standards of review.

In early 2003, over three years after Russell Means publicly announced the identities of the three people who murdered Ms. Aquash, the government apparently determined that the benefits of pursuing a trial for her murder outweighed the risks that such a trial would expose FBI misconduct. And, indeed, the trial did so. On February 4, 2004, nearly 28 years after the discovery of Aquash's lifeless body at the bottom of a 30-foot cliff just off a South Dakota State Highway running through the badlands, the government commenced the first trial for her murder by prosecuting Arlo Looking Cloud. The government elicited explosive hearsay testimony from Kamook Nichols-Ecoffey that Peltier told her and Aquash in graphic detail how he killed two FBI agents in the June 1975 shootout. She also testified that she heard Peltier call Aquash a snitch, which is the alleged motive for her murder. No evidence of FBI misconduct was presented at the trial.

As I wrote immediately after the trial of Arlo Looking Cloud concluded, the trial had little to do with Looking Cloud:

> A major occurrence in Rapid City last week. A trial, if that's what you want to call it. Many of you [the press] covered the murder trial of Arlo Looking Cloud. A 10-minute defense? Pretty sensational stuff.
>
> You didn't find what you were witnessing at all strange? I did. I mean, who was on trial?
>
> The majority of the testimony presented had nothing whatsoever to do with Arlo Looking Cloud, but prominent members of the American Indian Movement (AIM) and my client, Leonard Peltier, in particular. Leonard Peltier or the AIM leadership, I would remind you, are not on trial for the 1975 murder of Annie Mae Aquash. They have not been charged with the crime, either, simply because there is no evidence against them. Only rumor, conjecture, and innuendo.
>
> And that's all you were treated to in that courtroom this week. There was not one iota of proof presented to support many witnesses' "beliefs". And for every witness presented, there are any number of other individuals who could be called to appear and who would tell very different stories – that Annie Mae wasn't afraid of AIM, but the Federal Bureau of Investigation (FBI); she had stated this to various individuals on numerous occasions; and she had actually put such fears in writing. In 1975, she said she'd been told by investigators that she would be dead within the year if she didn't cooperate with FBI agents in framing AIM leaders and Leonard Peltier.

So, with Peltier having virtually no ability to seek release except for discretionary forms such as clemency and parole, the government decided to use the murder of Ms. Aquash against Peltier to try him for her murder in the court of public opinion. Now, the government could use the murder of Aquash to its benefit with very little to no risk of exposing misconduct by the FBI. Looking Cloud was already convicted, Graham stood to be tried and Theda Nelson Clarke allegedly suffered from Alzheimer's and/or some other related form of dementia.

Peltier's next parole hearing was to be held in 2009. The government ramped up its prosecutions in the murder of Ms. Aquash. In August of 2008, a grand jury indicted Vine Richard Marshall on charges of aiding and abetting in the murder, thereby raising again the allegations about Peltier and AIM leaders. In 2009, Thelma Rios pled guilty for her role in aiding and abetting the murder of Aquash. According to the plea agreement, she made the call to Denver to have Aquash detained and brought to Rapid City to face charges by AIM that she was a snitch. She allegedly did so at the behest of two AIM members whose names were redacted. It is widely opined that the redacted names were those of Lorelie Decora Means and Madonna Thunderhawk, relatives of Russell Means.

In 2010, Dick Marshall was acquitted of murder, while the government successfully convicted John Grahm of felony murder. Regardless of the results, the government reaffirmed its attack on Peltier and AIM and seemingly gained increased support in the court of public opinion.

Why did the government not pursue further people involved at that time? Why did the government not prosecute Theda Nelson Clarke, an undisputed ringleader of Aquash's murder, even though she was declared competent by two different judges in 2010? Why did the government not prosecute any one of the many other people implicated at the three trials? We will likely never know as a final grand jury investigation which commenced in the aftermath of Graham's trial resulted in no further indictments and in a closing of the investigation by the United States Attorney by 2014.

In this book, Dr. Wager identifies certain key issues which arose in connection with the Aquash murder trials and examines them in light of developing American legal philosophy. In doing so, he addresses, among other issues, the intertwining of two cases fraught with FBI misconduct: the investigation into the murder of Aquash and subsequent murder trials and its impact on the Peltier clemency attempts. In doing so, Dr. Wager provides unique insight into explaining what appears inexplicable by applying current legal philosophy to explain how the current American legal philosophies foster such governmental sleight of hand.

As the Tenth Circuit Court of appeals pronounced in 2003, it is undisputed that the government engaged in extreme misconduct to gain the conviction of Peltier. Yet, the Court lacked any power to address the misconduct. Now, nearly 50 years later, Peltier still sits in prison, many years longer than those charged with murder for that time period. Ironically, Peltier's efforts to seek clemency or parole will be impacted by the murder of Aquash which occurred nearly 50 years ago; a case initially fraught with FBI misconduct which now largely goes unnoticed and ignored. However, how the murder cases of Aquash are used to prosecute Peltier in the media is explained by analyzing the intersection of these cases considering current American legal philosophy.

Extremely significant is that this book is very timely. Peltier filed a new petition for clemency in 2021. Peltier's release has received strong support by Amnesty International, which has long espoused the unfairness of Peltier's trial and conviction, as well as prison treatment. On October 13, 2023, thirty-three Members of Congress sent a letter to President Biden requesting him to grant Executive Clemency to Peltier, citing what they said were the "prosecutorial misconduct" and "constitutional violations" that took place during Peltier's trial. As stated by United States Attorney James Reynolds, whose office handled the prosecution of Peltier, "His conviction and continued incarceration is a testament to a time and system of justice that no longer has a place in our society." Yet, as Dr. Wager discusses, current American legal theory continues to foster such results.

INTRODUCTION

Occurring during what has been widely referred to as a "Reign of Terror"[1] on Pine Ridge Indian Reservation, South Dakota, from 1973 to 1976, at least 75 murders of American Indians remain unsolved crimes today.[2] The Tribal President at the time, Richard A. "Dick" Wilson, notoriously oppressed his political adversaries using the brute and often deadly force of a policing group he formed, Guardians of the Oglala Nation (GOONs).[3]

Above all, Wilson and GOONs clashed with the American Indian Movement (AIM), a grassroots but militant organization of indigenous people from different recognized tribes throughout North America. Among its prominent members was Anna Mae Pictou-Aquash from the Mi'kmaq (also "Micmac") tribe of Nova Scotia,[4] murdered at age 30, presumably on Pine Ridge Reservation where her body was found in February 1976.[5]

The same month, Leonard Peltier,[6] another prominent AIM member, was arrested in Canada. He was eventually convicted in 1977 for the 1975 murders of two young FBI agents,[7] Ron Williams and Jack Coler.

According to FBI reports at the time, rumors had spread that Aquash had been killed not by Wilson's GOONs, but by members of AIM, because she had been an informant for the FBI, or even that while aggressively raising money, she had threatened prominent AIM members that she would turn over secrets to the FBI if they did not contribute money to various upcoming legal matters, including Peltier's.[8]

Over the years, as a popular movement formed to free Peltier through executive clemency,[9] the FBI's investigation of Aquash's murder intensified, but also began introducing new incriminating details about Peltier, such as how he himself had threatened Aquash with a gun in her mouth, as well as bragged openly to his close friends about executing the FBI agents he had always publically denied killing.[10]

More recent legal proceedings resulting in convictions against two AIM "foot soldiers"[11] purport to finally bring Aquash's murderers to justice, but raise more complex legal issues, as well as moral and factual dilemmas.

These dilemmas especially challenge American law but can also illustrate the value of continuing discussion by applying relevant thought from Continental Europe regarding interpretation, especially the ideas of Hans-Georg Gadamer (1900-2002), Paul Ricœur (1913-2005), and Jean-François Lyotard (1924-1998); likeminded jurists of the generation following them, including the Canadian Charles Taylor (b. 1931), the American Richard Rorty (1931-2007), and the Italian Gianni Vattimo (1936-2023); and others who have followed this discourse in recent years. When applied to now existing case law surrounding the Aquash murder, modern hermeneutical analysis combined with often contradictory postmodern perspective provides a bigger picture. What attempts to pass as tidy justice becomes only one side of a twisted reality.

More specifically, this advocating of legal hermeneutics revolves around two basic themes: 1) that legal hermeneutics is nothing new or even foreign to American law; and 2) that interpreting texts (statutes or opinions) relies on Aristotle's word "phronesis" (φρόνησις): a circumspect and improvised decision-making process. With this in mind, to claim that the ambiguous texts functioning as laws in America, many of them written by now dead jurists, should somehow nonetheless carry with them an unequivocal interpretation is to deny a longstanding tradition of interpreting texts in Western civilization.

American law has always relied generously on legal concepts difficult to define, such as "due process," "good faith," "fair play and substantial justice," or "the reasonable, prudent person." These tend to soften the otherwise harsh effects of a competition-driven society and its corresponding competition-driven jurisprudence with sometimes controversial winners.

Still, how do influences originally imported from Europe fare as an intellectual force in modern American law, which is driven by its own breed of chauvinist politics and one-upmanship? Legal educations are meticulous and ruthless merit systems derived out of attempts to measure natural intelligence as combined with a willing surrender to the work ethic. In legal practice, an adversarial system relies on two competing points of view often resolved in a potentially heated and highly dramatic contest with a winner determined by a neutral third party.

Longing for how rules govern American sports, most participants want a simple ruling so they can get on with the game. In this context, a law should be interpreted without fanfare or hemming and hawing, enforced the same way under any circumstances—a topic usually stemming from loftier, more universal concepts such as "the Rule of Law"[12] or "Natural Law."[13]

Unfortunately, the complete legal process with its lingering decisions has never been so simple. Sometimes the simplest of disputes leads to the most complex of legal quagmires. Nonetheless, recent legal philosophies such a "textualism"[14] lead some jurists to reexamine how laws are interpreted, perhaps hoping to disqualify some opposing philosophies along the way. These same jurists criticize what they feel are laws and opinions determined in some improperly spontaneous and even too sentimental application of immutable black-letter law.

In the same year as the Aquash murder, when Gadamer's *Wahrheit und Methode* appeared in English as *Truth and Method*,[15] a new and updated set of painstakingly articulate Continental ideas remarkably entered this give-and-take discussion as it existed in American law at a time when racial and gender issues were pressuring longstanding laws and procedures to be reevaluated and refurbished. It is important to take note of 1975, because although finally ending the Vietnam conflict changed dramatically the focus and resolve of the politically situated American Left, the countering American Right had still to reinvent itself. This reinvention of the American Right would eventually develop to represent similar breaks with traditional notions of judicial power and jurisdiction: the tax revolts of the late 1970s; the ensuing rise of Libertarianism; the rediscovery and zealous reapplication to politics of the writings of Ayn Rand[16]; and the election of Ronald Reagan in 1980, fueling a popularly perceived but decisive end to the Cold War and most of the lingering substantial sympathies in America for Marxism.[17] Reagan's revolution also included bringing out heavy legal artillery to specifically overturn *Roe v. Wade*[18] as well as instill and maintain suspicion about the Warren Court and its decision in *Brown v. Board of Education*.[19]

In other words, while the long murder mystery commenced surrounding a deceased Jane Doe on an Indian reservation in South Dakota later identified as Aquash, Gadamer had already introduced a new version of legal hermeneutics into a renewed American dialogue about the role of law and government in society. It all serendipitously occurred roughly at the same time as momentum was gaining for what was to become the

Neo-Conservative movement. This had found significant second wind in concepts such as "originalism" and "textualism" as represented loudly and forcefully by early voices such as Raoul Berger's (1901-2000)[20] and Robert Bork's (1927-2012).[21] In comparison, Gadamer's then still fresh and independent voice had already been inspiring its newly created English-speaking enthusiasts to reinvent what could be called a new form of "living constitutionalism,"[22] but now with a set of English words and articulations that had been translated from German. Representing understanding itself as something alive and living, not to be divorced robotically by an approach to interpreting texts as if they all had the same certainty and clarity as mathematical equations, a newly emerging American Left more quietly came into being.[23]

This inevitably led to a second generation of Gadamerian hermeneuts (e.g., Taylor, Rorty, and Vattimo) who championed a renewal of criticism of interpretation in law, especially as it might pertain to American law during and after the Neo-Conservative movement.[24] It also brought forth a new third generation. How Gadamer's ideas might ultimately be employed currently[25] requires summation of what has been reinvention upon reinvention of this debate about interpretation. More recent decisions involving homosexuality and gender preference[26] make the matter especially pressing. Although basically the same as formulated in the 1970s, the argument that legal hermeneutics plays an essential and crucial role in American law requires continuous modification but steadfast continuity.

Postmodernism helps continue the discussion, but with some more drastic analytical maneuvers. Even younger minds, especially those of Steven Best (b. 1955), and Douglas Kellner (b. 1943), have broken new ground in these areas in more recent years. In this way, the second chapter of this book, which examines the status and influence of legal hermeneutics in modern American law, continues in the third chapter by concentrating on postmodernism.

There is no wide consensus as to what postmodernism definitively entails or represents and, even more than hermeneutics, it is nonetheless applied as a rubric to define current trends in thinking and activity from as diverse disciplines as art and architecture to history and philosophy. Attempting to definitively define what postmodernism is; when it became recognized as an important trend of the late 20th-century; or what its limitations and opponents might be; may prove to be an even more difficult and elusive task than determining such boundaries for modernism itself or its relevance to the Neo-Conservative.

Suffice it to say, on the other hand, that it is not necessary to define modernism before defining postmodernism based on the free usage both words still enjoy in the context of today's intellectual discourse. However, attempting to define these articulations now that there has been a period of time that could appropriately be considered an opened-and-closed era of postmodernism (whether actually continuing or ending as such, or ended long ago) allows the definition to be a more descriptive than normative task: the questions "what is modernism" and "what is postmodernism" now have a body of examples out of history to draw from.

Yet for the purpose of an example chosen to illustrate this pregnant moment in history, Aquash's murder especially helps keep relevant concepts alive with the extensiveness of both its legal and factual dilemmas. American legal hermeneutics would by definition even require thorough analysis as to how and why justice for Aquash cannot rest on its vigorous but irresolute legal process.

CHAPTER ONE

THREE FOCAL POINTS

This study cannot exhaustively examine all dilemmas of the Anna Mae Pictou-Aquash murder case, let alone conclusively solve any of them. Some are touched upon and implied in the Introduction, but at least three broad issues potent for further discussion and legal analysis help to illustrate why this complex murder case continues to tug at the very fibers that keep American jurisprudence consistently enforced and respected, let alone how it ranks in importance inside the well-established canon of Federal American Indian law.

This first chapter develops three broad issues, or "focal points," based on the facts and litigation that have come to fore in the almost 50-year controversy surrounding the Aquash murder: 1) Federal and state criminal jurisdiction involving American Indians; 2) reassessing the facts of both the Aquash and Leonard Peltier cases for the purpose of a more accurate overview necessary to evaluate the legal outcomes; and 3) a brief nod to postmodernism as a recent method of ultimately analyzing and smoothing over specific contradictions involving Federal American Indian law.

First, the criminal jurisdiction issues raised in the Aquash murder are so unusual and therefore brittle in terms of how they were resolved, that the analysis requires both a thorough examination of the official narrative and a careful analysis of four subtopics (sufficiency of an indictment; situs of a crime; extradition of indigenous people in general; and determining the identity of indigenous people). In summing this up, the issue is ultimately framed in the following way: in a murder case on Indian Territory involving a defendant and victim who are "First Nation" Canadian citizens (i.e., North American Indians recognized according to the laws of Canada, but not necessarily by the United States), can a Federal court of the United States nonetheless determine that such Canadian citizens belong to Federally recognized Indian Tribes making them subject to Federal criminal jurisdiction upon extradition?

Second, this case piggybacks on another prominent case, not necessarily the double homicide itself that Aquash's associate Peltier was convicted of in 1977, but certainly on the ongoing well-organized campaign for Peltier's executive clemency, as well as the FBI's counter-campaign to make sure he does not get clemency. The high-strung politics pitting the FBI and several other police organizations (Indian or otherwise) against AIM continue to produce rumors, disinformation, and damage control surrounding what was essentially an armed insurrection suppressed with deadly force. Determining the facts in such a context requires painstaking assessment outside the narrative of the legal proceedings.

Finally, an afterthought suggests why trends of postmodernism in Federal Indian Law to deal with these troubling facts have already occurred. Because Federal Indian Law deals with a minority population striving to preserve its original culture, not assimilation into the majority culture (at least not anymore), contradictions and exceptions have little other legal argument backing them up than it simply must be this way, even though the law says it should be another way. Put simply, can postmodern interpretation of the facts and motives in this murder of an AIM activist at a critical time in history create a more complete and just model of the reality at hand?

FOCAL POINT ONE: CRIMINAL JURISDICTIONS

On February 24, 1976, around 2 P.M., a rancher found a dead human body on his land while tending livestock.[27] According to his own description, it lay at the bottom of a 30-foot cliff, 100 feet away from South Dakota State Highway 73, about 10 miles east of Wanblee, and 18 miles south of Kadoka.[28] This location in South Dakota is indisputably within the borders of Pine Ridge Indian Reservation.[29]

At first, the female body was declared an unidentified Jane Doe,[30] and the official cause of death after an autopsy was exposure.[31] At the request of FBI investigators present, the coroner then cut off her hands, which were kept for several days until after the body was buried before being sent to the FBI's laboratory in Washington D.C. for fingerprint analysis.[32]

On March 5, the FBI lab identified the fingerprints as Aquash's.[33] Demands by AIM's lawyer and Aquash's sister to exhume the body from the local cemetery[34] led to a reexamination of the remains, notably x-rays of the head, which determined Aquash had actually suffered a close-range gunshot wound to the back of the head.[35] The bullet was still lodged in the skull, near the left temple.[36]

In 2003, more than 25 years after the homicide, a Federal grand jury indicted Fritz Arlo Looking Cloud and John "John Boy Patton" Graham for the premeditated murder of Aquash.[37] Federal jurisdiction for the grand jury over the crime was appropriate by mention of the Major Crimes Act,[38] as well as mentioning Federal statutes for aiding and abetting[39] and murder.[40] Although the Major Crimes Act requires that the perpetrator must be an Indian who commits the crime on Indian Territory before there is Federal jurisdiction, the indictment only specifically identified Looking Cloud as an Indian.[41] Graham was in Canada in 2003 requiring extradition, but Looking Cloud was arrested in Denver to stand trial.[42]

The trials of Looking Cloud, Richard Marshall, and Graham determined the following as facts: Aquash had been staying in Denver with Theda Nelson Clarke[43] (at the home of Troy Lynn Yellow Wood) both as a guest and fugitive from the law in late November, 1975[44]; before Thanksgiving, some AIM members in Denver met informally at Yellow Wood's house with a few prominent members of the Chicano organization Crusade for Justice, and there was discussion about Aquash's fate for being an informant[45]; for reasons still undetermined, Clarke then procured the assistance of two young male "guards" (Looking Cloud and Graham) and in essence "took custody" of Aquash in the cellar, eventually transporting her on December 10 with the two guards to Rapid City, South Dakota, in the back of her Ford Pinto hatchback[46]; the four arrived in Rapid City after a six-hour drive from Denver and managed to enter an empty apartment where they spent the rest of the night[47]; Aquash was seen sometime in mid-December at the offices of the Wounded Knee Legal Defense/Offense Committee (WKLD/OC) in Rapid City with prominent members of AIM, but without the company of Clarke or her foot soldiers[48]; on December 11, Clarke and her foot soldiers attempted to take Aquash to the home of AIM activist Vine Richard Marshall and his family in Allen, South Dakota, but he ultimately did not allow them to stay there[49]; the four later drove to the home of Bill Means on the Rosebud Reservation, but did not stay there either[50]; later that evening, Aquash was driven to a cliff off of Highway 73 and shot in the back of the head by Graham on direct orders from Clarke[51]; after the execution, Graham handed the gun to Looking Cloud, who claims he also feared for his life and in turn emptied the gun, firing all the remaining bullets into the ground[52]; and Clarke disposed of the gun used to kill Aquash under a bridge that Looking Cloud later led authorities to, but the weapon was never recovered.[53] Looking Cloud was found guilty of first degree murder and sentenced to life in prison.[54] The Eighth Circuit affirmed his conviction and life sentence.[55]

In 2007, Graham was finally extradited from Canada to face charges for Aquash's murder.[56] Anticipating jurisdictional issues regarding the Indian identities of both Graham and Aquash, a second grand jury issued a superseding indictment in 2008 with three counts,[57] although pretrial motions to dismiss both indictments was eventually granted.[58] The three similarly worded counts in the 2008 indictment invoke the following statutes: the first alleging Graham is an Indian and subject to Federal jurisdiction under 18 U.S.C. § 1153 (2006)[59]; the second alleging Aquash is an Indian, making Graham subject to Federal jurisdiction under 18 U.S.C. § 1152 (2006)[60]; and the third almost identical to the 2003 indictment without alleging Graham and Aquash were Indians.[61]

While still in South Dakota on September 9, 2009, Graham was indicted by a Pennington County, South Dakota, grand jury on two state charges: kidnapping resulting in death; and premeditated murder.[62] Even though found not guilty on the premeditated murder charge, he was convicted of felony-murder kidnapping on December 10, 2010, and sentenced to life in prison on January 24, 2011.[63] His conviction was upheld by the South Dakota Supreme Court on May 30, 2012.[64] A writ of habeas corpus is planned.[65] A 2018 appeal to the 8th Circuit also failed.

Often described as a "jurisdictional maze,"[66] options available in Federal Indian law to prosecute Graham required careful planning by prosecutors.[67] Initially, a sound strategy should have been prepared to explain why Federal jurisdiction, not state or even tribal jurisdictions, was appropriate for a crime on an Indian reservation involving at least one recognized Indian. The U.S. Attorney for South Dakota at the time, James E. McMahon, nonetheless proceeded against both Looking Cloud and Graham using only the following language of the 2003 first indictment:

> "On or about the 12th day of December, 1975, near Wanblee, in Indian Country, in the District of South Dakota, the defendants, Fritz Arlo Looking Cloud, an Indian, and John Graham, a/k/a/ John Boy Patton, willfully, deliberately, maliciously, and with premeditation and malice aforethought, did unlawfully kill and aid and abet the unlawful killing of Annie Mae Aquash, a/k/a Annie Mae Pictou, by shooting her with a firearm, in violation of 18 U.S.C. §§ 1111, 1153, and 2."[68]

A planned defense that both Canadians, Graham and Aquash, were not Federally recognized Indians and therefore Graham was not subject to Federal jurisdiction was obviously thought to have been overcome by mention of § 2, aiding and abetting,[69] but ultimately needed the support of the second, superseding indictment in 2008, once Looking Cloud was in prison and his case was concluded. Under the guidance of McMahon's successor, Marty J. Jackley, this superseding 2008 indictment argued its three almost identically worded counts in the alternative.[70] In retrospect, these two strategies were only successful in that it got Graham extradited and eventually under the jurisdiction of state court.

In retrospect, the counterintuitive legal theory that Graham and Aquash are not Indians raises relevant issues about the way this matter navigated the criminal jurisdictional maze for Indians on Indian Territory. Analyzing further the following subtopics helps focus on these issues: 1) are Federal indictments for crimes on Indian Territory sufficient if Indian identities of perpetrator(s) or victim(s) are not mentioned?; 2) how should the situs of the crime on Indian Territory be properly analyzed?; 3) are Indians properly extradited without notice to their Tribes or First Nations?; and 4) can the Indian identities of Canadian Indians ever be recognized by the United States?

1. Sufficiency

In light of extensive analysis of the Indian identities of Graham and Aquash in a brief by the United States answering Graham's motion to dismiss,[71] the United States also expressed confidence it could preserve the original 2003 indictment by stating both that aiding and abetting an Indian (Looking Cloud or even Clarke, Thelma Rios, and Marshall) was enough to invoke Federal jurisdiction,[72] and that proving Indian identity could be determined during trial without having to allege it on the indictment, because Graham would have had "notice" of the Indian identity issue.[73] In the end, the district court granted so-called "interlocutory dismissal" of both the 2003 indictment and the third count of the 2008 indictment[74] against Graham.[75] The United States appealed this decision to the Eighth Circuit, which affirmed the lower court by and large for the same reasons.[76] Then state jurisdiction took over the prosecution of Graham as a non-Indian.[77] The United States did not reconvene a grand jury, so the Indian identity issue for Canadians like Graham and Aquash was probably finally deemed too risky and complicated to continue.[78]

It has long been established that for crimes allegedly committed in Indian Territory, a Federal indictment is insufficient unless it states clearly that the accused, victim, or both is/are an Indian(s).[79] It is ultimately a violation of the 5th Amendment right to a grand jury if no Indian race is

11

specified on such an indictment under 18 U.S.C. §§ 1152 or 1153.[80] These elements of the crime must be explicitly affirmed by the grand jury and proven by the trier-of-fact like all other elements of the crime beyond a reasonable doubt.[81] Jurisdiction based on the identity of the accused and victim of the crime can be raised any time.[82]

The United States relied on *Pemberton* and *United States v. White Horse*[83] to preserve the indictments, which did not sway either the district court or Eighth Circuit. In fact, the Eighth Circuit also cited *Norquay*,[84] which specifically held that the Major Crimes Act cannot use accomplice liability to include a non-Indian accomplice.[85]

In the end, Graham prevailed at the Federal level.[86] The State of South Dakota then stepped in to serve Graham since he had already been conveniently extradited from Canada and was therefore physically present in the state.[87] Because the state charges were based on events outside Pine Ridge Indian Reservation, they did not entail proving Indian identity or how that issue should appear on the face of an indictment.[88]

2. Situs

In the Looking Cloud trial and appeal, the jury essentially determined that Aquash was murdered near a state highway not far on a horizontal plane from the area where the body was found, even though the theory that the body may have been dumped there after being murdered elsewhere, possibly off the reservation, was never argued.[89] These facts now stand if deference to the Looking Cloud and Graham courts is upheld. The judges in those cases also had to determine as a matter of law, that Amiotte's ranch was in Indian Territory.[90] Both situs elements, location of crime and status of Indian Territory, determine subject matter jurisdiction of the Federal court and can be raised at any time in a Federal proceeding.[91] The fact that the situs was near a right of way is also explicitly accounted for in the statute.[92]

Amiotte testified that the land his ranch is on is held in trust for an individual.[93] Sufficing for a legal ruling of "Indian Territory," the trust relationship with the Federal government is not atypical and was easily determined as a matter of law.[94]

Blood under the head of the dead body suggested death occurred where the body was found.[95] On the other hand, hair still embedded in the side of the cliff suggested she may have fallen from the cliff, possibly lifeless. There was not evidence at the top of the cliff that a gun was discharged there or that any bleeding took place there.[96]

Nonetheless, the trier of fact in both Looking Cloud and Graham trials held that there was enough information to conclude beyond a reasonable doubt that the victim died at the scene.[97] Precisely what details convinced both juries is not specifically stated in the opinions, or what theories were considered.

3. Extradition

As for extradition issues, Graham's defense against state jurisdiction relied mostly on the Doctrine of Specialty,[98] which ultimately did not apply because the Canadian justice minister had provided the prosecution with a sealed affidavit, waiving Canada's rights as an asylum state.[99] The only other extradition issue was raised marginally by an affidavit submitted to the Canadian court from a Chief of the Squamish Nation, who claimed to have recognized Graham as Squamish, giving him a Squamish name ("Sahd leetz"): whether Tribes or First Nations have sovereign powers when one of their members is extradited to a jurisdiction within the United States or some other foreign government.[100]

Even if the U.S. Constitution's extradition language only dealt with the states,[101] as did a corresponding statute,[102] treaties between the United States and Indians sometimes had extradition agreements written into them.[103] This supports the argument that tribal courts' claims to extradition rights are valid,[104] as does cases, such as *Arizona ex rel. Merrill v. Turtle*,[105] in which the rights of tribes to have their own extradition rules were respected. On the other hand, in *State v. Spotted Horse*,[106] South Dakota took note of a lack of an extradition clause in the Tribal Constitution from the Standing Rock Reservation where Spotted Horse was apprehended, which allowed his arrest without any extradition issues.[107]

The Squamish Chief's request was not unexpectedly ignored by both Federal and South Dakota courts. Still, however small this Chief's voice, the legal issue resounds and ought to have been addressed.

4. Identity

Although Graham's defense at the Federal level was emphatic denial that he and Aquash were Indians,[108] the State of South Dakota bypassed all Indian Territory issues by basing its charges on events off the reservation.[109] Still, the United States had prepared to argue that both Graham and Aquash were Indians based on the longstanding two-prong *Rogers* test[110]: 1) some Indian blood; and 2) otherwise recognized as an Indian. Meanwhile, a proposed Indian identity statute, 18 USC § 1150[111] would have solved the problem of what to do with Indians only recognized in Canada and Mexico.[112]

As for the problem with Graham and Aquash, only the first prong is at issue, because various cultural activities on Pine Ridge Reservation should have satisfied the second prong. As for the first prong, any "Tribes" they would have been born into, giving them the appropriate blood, do not appear on the list of Federally recognized Indians.[113] On the other hand, the United States did not exhaustively search for variations of the bloodlines that might have helped their case. For example, Graham's First Nation, the Southern Tutchone,[114] is still part of the larger lingual family of Athabaskan, which the United States has recognized in Alaska.[115]

As far as Aquash and the Mi'kmaq are concerned, the first treaty with Indians after the Declaration of Independence in 1776 was with the Mi'kmaq, known as the Treaty of Watertown.[116] Efforts to show this as Federal recognition of the Mi'kmaq have failed in the past,[117] based on the fact that this treaty was before the U.S. Constitution and was technically only between the Mi'kmaq and the Commonwealth of Massachusetts.[118] Nonetheless, the argument might have merit when considered liberally within the so-called Indian "canons of construction,"[119] along with the fact that the United States officially recognizes the Aroostock Band of Micmacs, which are a branch of the group Aquash belonged to and part of the greater Wabanaki Confederation of Tribes.[120]

The United States probably still cannot overcome the *Rogers* test applied to both Graham and Aquash, even if a new indictment were issued, but if it could, dual sovereignty[121] would allow a Federal district court to continue its prosecutions against Graham despite the state conviction, if Indian identity could ever be resolved.

FOCAL POINT TWO: REASSESSING THE FACTS

Whether by intention or not, the convictions of Looking Cloud and Graham actually serve to keep a tenuous relevance between Aquash's murder and the ongoing Peltier controversy, where Aquash's murder has always lingered as an ancillary issue. Because of the now well-documented way in which much of the evidence against Peltier was fraudulently created by the FBI,[122] a neutral observer might at first suspect the same aggressive and perhaps dishonest police work might have occurred to build the cases against Aquash's now convicted assailants, Looking Cloud and Graham. This certainly creates a suspicion for which further assessment, if possible, of the facts are in order.

The FBI's ardent zeal in maintaining justice for the deaths of two of its young agents has morphed into an all-out campaign against executive clemency for Peltier. That makes an extra piece of otherwise irrelevant evidence in the Graham trial (which depicts Peltier bragging that he actually did kill the agents[123]) fuel further controversy.

Clearly, both the FBI and AIM have now adopted Aquash as its cause's martyr. For the FBI and its allies, she serves as an example of how violent and ruthless AIM actually was, unbeknownst to or perhaps unfairly ignored by Peltier's liberal followers who mostly insist AIM is ultimately advocating a just solution to the unjust treatment of American Indians in the United States. For AIM, Aquash serves as an example of how violent and ruthless the FBI and its allies were during the Reign of Terror on the Pine Ridge Indian Reservation, as well as both how gory this violence could be and indiscriminate in terms of how it extended to women[124] and children.

Appropriately, Aquash remains a salient candidate for martyrdom to any cause, because in retrospect nothing that she was known to be involved with would in the least way distinguish her from others in this scenario to such an extent that either side should take such trouble to have her marked for death. The ongoing rumors that she was a snitch—whether from any actual collaboration with the FBI; an irrational belief by AIM members; or the result of the FBI's alleged methods of making someone appear to be an informant ("snitch-jacketing")—hardly amount to actually going through with the great risk and moral sacrifice of a formal execution.

One of the earliest theories, that she was simply one more victim of random violence on the Reservation, had been the easiest, default theory among AIM supporters until the convictions of Looking Cloud and Graham. Other conspiracy theories involving some unknown element serving as the motive to kill her, such as she knew something that she was not supposed to know (what she knew about Peltier or some FBI secret), remain high conjecture with little evidence.

A patient historian is left to pick up the pieces of this now almost 50-year murder mystery and high-profile political issue.[125] Suffice it to say, the convictions against Looking Cloud and Graham have most probably not settled the matter, which will continue to spawn theories from both sides. After all, these two very minor AIM foot soldiers were both at the most doing little else than carrying out orders within a chain of command that found them taking orders from an unstable woman. Even if Looking Cloud and Graham were rightly convicted of aiding and abetting in this murder, who else should be responsible, especially for giving such orders to Theda Clarke?

Although nonetheless pressing issues, these concerns can only be presented here with broad strokes, because the facts have now become decades old and run the risk of vast distortion. The issues surrounding both Peltier and Aquash also tend to strip away any semblance of political unrest on the Indian reservation, suggesting that both the FBI and AIM were engaged in a petty, personal squabble. As naïve as it might at first appear, reminding the reader of the context of how political and armed insurrections very typically produce casualties emphasizes a crucial element in these controversies. First, examining the ultimate motives of the FBI should be placed in the context of all these questions. In light of that, Aquash's case next should then also be placed in the context of the AIM point of view and its possible motives for using deadly force. Third, one more abbreviated overview of the Peltier conviction should help shed light on some of these possible motives from both the FBI and AIM. And, finally, a synthesis of all these aspects into the facts of the Aquash case might help give the closest thing to a definitive version of the murder possible here, even if conjecture remains high and unknown factors remain unsolvable without more evidence.

1. FBI Motives for Deceptive Tactics

Some of the most pressing motives of the FBI relevant to its cases against Peltier, Looking Cloud, and Graham, break into three basic categories: 1) maintaining the special reputation of the FBI, in that its elite status depends on inciting fear among criminals so that any resistance, let alone resistance using deadly force, will undoubtedly be met with power so forceful (if not at times even unlawful), that the "bad guys" will never prevail; 2) preventing AIM from instigating a full blown insurrection on the Pine Ridge Indian Reservation in light of the 1973 71-day siege of Wounded Knee; and 3) making a personal retribution following the deaths of Agents Coler and Williams, not to mention acquittals in the first trial on self defense. Although specifying and examining such motives may be unusual in a legal analysis, a good part of the confusion surrounding this case stems from the FBI's expert public relations and the remarkable ability of its agents to make statements that fend off any accusations that they did anything improper. A good example of this comes from Douglas J. Domin, one of the former Special Agents in Charge of the regional FBI office in Minneapolis:

"We were trying to do our job, which was a very difficult one, on the reservations. And we did that the best we could, and I'm sure we had some missteps, but our heart was pure and our work was good."[126]

In direct contrast to this innocent plea of understanding is the more direct approach in Joseph H. Trimbach's book.[127] No other voice relevant to the FBI point of view here is louder and more voluble. Trimbach also served as the Special Agent in Charge of the regional FBI office in Minneapolis during the killings of Coler, Williams, Joe Stuntz, Aquash, and the Reign of Terror, although he repeatedly states in the book that the "Reign of Terror" was an exaggeration.[128] Trimbach basically denies that those agents working in the FBI at that time were anything but heroes, and that Richard Wilson's GOONs were doing anything but properly maintaining order. Reading Trimbach's book brings pleasure and comfort to anyone who believes that Peltier is a ruthless murderer and was guilty all along; the trial of Darrelle "Dino" Butler and Bob Robideau was a farce; Judge Gerald Heaney of the Eighth Circuit inappropriately recommended clemency for Peltier[129]; or that the FBI is a shining and all but infallible organization that assiduously respects the Constitutional rights of all American citizens.

In light of the first of the three FBI motives examined here, Trimbach supplies probably the best anecdote illustrating the necessity of keeping the FBI's rough and tumble reputation as an elite policing power.[130] He tells the story from early in his career of capturing three escaped convicts in a Florida hotel who were armed and deadly, but did not make a stand because they did not want to "mess with the FBI."[131] Robideau expresses almost exactly the same sentiments as the escaped convicts in Trimbach's story:

"...we already accepted the fact that, ah, we were dead. I mean, when you hear the stories or look at movies about the FBI, you know, they always get their man."[132]

Trimbach's stories are even part of a larger genre of fictionalized accounts of real events emphasizing how police forces gain respect from the outlaws they are chasing if they play fast and easy with the rules themselves.[133] Even though this might be scandalous to the general law-abiding citizens and bring the FBI legal troubles later on should their arrestee find a good defense attorney who knows how to expose the unlawfulness, some readers undoubtedly will find Trimbach's romantic notion difficult to resist.[134]

Because of this blatant romanticization, Trimbach has definite problems making fine distinctions in his book, resorting to downright ranting and name-calling[135] when attacking someone that might criticize the FBI's policies. For example, when discussing one of AIM's strongest arguments against the FBI's tactics, that is, the fraudulent affidavits by Myrtle Poor Bear to gain Peltier's extradition from Canada, Trimbach complains that somehow it was actually AIM, not the FBI, who used threats and intimidation against her without indicating anything specific.[136] Meanwhile, Poor Bear has made several filmed interviews where she appears to be speaking freely claiming that she never knew Peltier, even though the affidavits prepared with the help of the FBI claim she was his girlfriend; she was not at the Jumping Bull Compound when the shooting occurred; the FBI threatened to interfere with custody over her daughter, Mardi; and these threats induced her to lie in the affidavits about knowing Peltier or witnessing anything about the shooting of Coler and Williams.[137] Although Judge Heaney called this FBI tactic a "disgrace" on national television,[138] Trimbach repeatedly denies that there was ever anything improper about the way the FBI built its case against Peltier using these Poor Bear affidavits.[139] Unfortunately, this suggests there actually is something improper about the case against Peltier, and pronounced pressure from a highly skeptical element within the civilian population is entirely justified.

Trimbach still makes a deliberately caustic and provocative irony in the title of his book when he refers to AIM as a "Mafia." Of course, reference to the famous Italian Mafia in the United States insults AIM's otherwise just cause of making right the injustices done against American Indians, because the Italian Mafia in America would scarcely have anything to do with public demonstrations such as sit-ins or forcefully occupying Government land. On the other hand, Trimbach's point is that AIM was a militant organization that did not hesitate to use violence in the machinations that were its own ruthless politics and struggles for power within its own organization. This point must be driven home if a reader is ever to fairly consider that AIM itself was responsible for the murder of Aquash.

Although AIM certainly was not dedicated to the same vows of non-violence that Mahatma Gandhi or Rev. Martin Luther King, Jr. employed, there was certainly a kinship between AIM and other leftwing political organizations especially during the 1960s and 1970s that did not hesitate to use militant tactics: the Black Panther Party, the Weather Underground Organization, and a number of organizations around the world similarly using strategically armed insurrections and revolution to ultimately challenge the policies of unstable governments. Whether subtly or blatantly devoted to Marxism, such movements were certainly not Mafias, in the sense of using violent means and ethnicity for wealth and power, but actually gained respectability from America's nonviolent left—especially certain movie personalities such as Marlon Brando or Peter Coyote—as necessarily fighting "fire with fire" in dealing with what were typically violent and unjust authorities suppressing them.

The case of Nelson Mandela (1918-2013) demonstrates that another of these violent organizations, the African National Congress, not only elevated its leader to a respectable President of the government it was fighting, but also to a worldwide symbol of civility and world peace. Of course, there is still a vast difference between Mandela, who was a self-taught lawyer educated in the way of the white race oppressing him, and AIM, which is by and large made up of uneducated members with sympathies for the traditional way of life of their ancestors.[140]

Meanwhile, the FBI had the task of not only combating the violent militancy of the Italian Mafia in America, as well as other politically rightwing organizations such as the Ku Klux Klan, but also violent militancy from the American Left. Even before the 71-day standoff at Wounded Knee in 1973, AIM's reputation for occupying Government land had reached a breaking point, probably inciting orders from within the Nixon Administration itself, as AIM-leader John Trudell himself admits:

> "In 1972 during the Nixon re-election, we went to DC, and we ended up occupying the Bureau of Indian Affairs National Headquarters. We kept it for like a week, but it was highly embarrassing to the Nixon Administration, you know. We had gone too far."[141]

Keeping in mind that the seven-day occupation of Bureau of Indian Affairs (BIA) National Headquarters indeed was a disruptive act of trespassing, there was still never any harm to people either actual or intended. Probably as much as if not more than the Wounded Knee occupation three months later,[142] this occupation fanned the flames that would eventually lead to FBI involvement with the escalated violence from the BIA police force on the Pine Ridge Indian Reservation.[143]

In light of the impasse[144] to the Wounded Knee occupation on the watch of the newly reelected Nixon Administration, the FBI certainly had reason to plan for a contingency that AIM would plan another occupation, even if the cost of Wounded Knee was great on the AIM side of the issue. Although the FBI's now famous COINTELPRO, which involved sending spies into suspicious domestic organizations was then formerly defunct as an official program,[145] an FBI spy named Douglas Durham successfully infiltrated AIM.[146] Because the Wounded Knee impasse involved a negotiated end, at least a line of communication between the FBI and AIM leaders Dennis Banks and Russell Means had tentatively been formed.[147] All of these facts reflect what was probably the most important and prevalent activity of the FBI, which was basic intelligence gathering. Even in this capacity, this intelligence gathering was secret and led to the sort of paranoia among AIM members that led them to believe Aquash was an informant.

The final motivation behind the FBI other than their overall tough reputation and specific secret tasks on the Pine Ridge Indian Reservation involved deeply personal feelings that its agents had for fallen colleagues. Coler and Williams were agents in their late 20s and the ignoble way they were killed created bitter resentment within the ranks of the FBI. Coler's widow, who was not trained professionally to make public statements about the death of her husband, nonetheless stated her frustration succinctly as follows:

> "And I would love to talk to somebody who could really tell me what really, really happened that day. Someone who wasn't involved in the shooting, somebody who knows the truth. I would love to hear the real story."[148]

As much as only the most coldhearted would ever doubt the genuineness of her sentiments and the needs of the other agents for punishing someone for this crime, this statement also reflects that no one except the actual killers know (or knew) what happened and that reasonable doubt of Peltier's guilt still exists, even if he were indeed the actual killer.

2. AIM Motives for Deceptive Tactics

AIM's motives for deception break into the following categories: 1) general fear and paranoia stemming from extreme tactics from Federal and local policing organizations; 2) its own sort of strategic political posturing in light of the general public's sympathies, especially for clemency for Peltier; and 3) maintaining discipline and the reputation of strength that comes from organizing a revolutionary organization at the grassroots level. All of these motives are aptly illustrated in one specific example involving one of Peltier's prosecutors, former Congressman and Governor

William Janklow (1939-2012), which will serve as a lurid example at the end of this analysis.

Aside from the often random and intimidating deadly violence from GOONs, which is now well documented although almost entirely without legal remedy to the victims, AIM members were typically and certainly aware that the FBI was spying on them. In fact, the espionage tactic of "snitch-jacketing," which involved keeping your opponents confused and disorganized by creating false suspicion that one of their members was a spy, was something that some Aquash theorists speculated created the motive behind killing her.[149]

Rumors abounded that AIM members were so suspicious of Aquash being an informer, that they were all but holding her prisoner within the small fugitive AIM group that escaped to the Pacific Northwest in Marlon Brando's Winnebago.[150] These unsubstantiated rumors of Aquash being a virtual prisoner all this time even include a story that the senior AIM members forced her to work on explosives with the idea that when they were used, her fingerprints would be on the equipment, falsely framing her for the deed.[151]

Aside from such paranoia, AIM members also wove theories of Federal and local policing forces deliberately planning to eradicate AIM through various tactics. For example, Banks has always held that Coler and Williams were part of a larger FBI conspiracy, and the day they died, they were to raid the "Tent City" near the Jumping Bull Compound where Peltier, Butler and Robideau were and essentially assassinate them:

> "The FBI declared war on the American Indian Movement. They don't run in with guns into a community shooting at people and not expect to get hurt…. They came to fight the American Indian Movement. They didn't come to serve a warrant. They came to kill people that day. They came to hurt people."[152]

Although it is highly unlikely that any such methodical raid by the FBI would include exposing two young agents acting as assassins to such danger that they would be killed as they actually were, AIM members had good grounds to question the cover story that Coler and Williams were serving a warrant on an American Indian named Jimmy Eagle for stealing a pair of cowboy boots.[153]

No matter how genuine the suspicions of AIM has been over the years, they have certainly played their own sort of public relations game and collaborated to create their own spin on stubbornly missing facts. One of the most important stories that often is now left out of the Peltier discussion involves an addendum to Peter Matthiessen's book, *In the Spirit of Crazy Horse*, and a character known only as "Mr. X."[154] Matthiessen interviewed a man in disguise who conveniently filled in all the holes of this story: Mr. X and two colleagues were delivering dynamite to AIM; they were riding in a "red vehicle," as described in all the FBI agents' radio broadcasts[155]; the pickup filled with explosives was to make a delivery to the Tent City; the agents followed the pickup as it was turning onto Jumping Bull Compound; Mr. X and companions brandished weapons, making the agents think they were going to shoot; the agents shot first; as the firefight started, Mr. X feared bullets would hit the explosives so drove the pickup away from the firefight; once the agents were wounded, Mr. X returned to the scene to examine the situation; Agent Williams raised his gun on Mr. X and purely in self-defense, Mr. X shot him dead; and purely by reflex, Mr. X turned to shoot the otherwise dying Agent Coler, twice.[156] Even though this story was always considered unverified,[157] Robideau adopted it as an ultimate alibi,[158] with both he and Peltier claiming they knew who the real killer was, but could not reveal his identity out of loyalty to AIM.[159] Butler now claims that this Mr. X story was a deliberate hoax propagated by Robideau.[160] Apparently, the Mr. X story is largely abandoned by Peltier, whose latest known version of the event is that he simply "does not know who killed the agents and doesn't want to know."[161]

As much as the ultimate demise of the Mr. X story certainly suggests that prominent AIM members are able and willing to spin the facts and play a deceptive public relations game, Butler also claims he refused to go along with the Mr. X story because, in essence, the truth was on AIM's side and therefore AIM did not need to resort to such things.[162] If the AIM members were to try and spin a false alibi, it might have been convenient for them to blame the shootings on Joe Stuntz, who was killed at the scene and therefore could tell no more stories. Instead, the AIM version of the event suggests that someone outside of its Tent City shot the agents. This leaves many questions about the general nature of the AIM organization in its willingness and ability to keep secrets and how members could have carried out the execution of Aquash and kept it a secret for decades.

Interestingly enough, Trimbach goes to great lengths to criticize Peltier attorney Barry Bachrach, calling him "a big-mouthed officer of the court"[163] for calling the litigation against Looking Cloud and Graham a "set-up" and as being yet another way of "getting more shots in at Leonard."[164] Today, Bachrach believes the case against AIM's involvement in killing Aquash has been proven beyond a reasonable doubt, although he still questions why Clarke, who he claims was not as mentally unstable as reported, was not charged as well.[165]

Other theorists, even from the Indian traditionalists' point of view such as Janis Schmidt, also have no trouble believing that the AIM leadership, including Banks, Means, Clyde Bellencourt, and Trudell, have never hesitated to use deadly violence to get things done.[166] Schmidt is quick however not to absolve the FBI of its improper role in the Reign of Terror and even using the truce agreement of the Wounded Knee standoff as a sort of ongoing collaboration between the FBI and AIM, which has been invoked in such a way as to continue to manage the standoff situation on the Pine Ridge Reservation.

Oddly enough, Banks had an extramarital affair with Aquash and still claims that she was the love of his life.[167] Bank's wife at the time, Ka-mook Nichols, who was a good friend of Aquash, since became involved with Hollywood movies and actually had a romantic relationship with Robert Ecoffey, the FBI investigator who put together the case against Looking Cloud, with the help of his own spy Richard Two Elk.[168] When Nichols testified at Looking Cloud's trial, she dropped a bombshell when claiming that Peltier admitted to her, as well as Aquash and Nichols's sister Bernie Lafferty, that he was the one who executed the FBI agents and showed no remorse.[169] Trimbach certainly makes hay of this, including Lafferty's confirmation of such a confession, claiming that this resolves the case against Peltier once and for all,[170] even if Peltier has never been allowed to confront these accusers and this nonmaterial fact was inserted into the Looking Cloud trial.[171] Peltier's "confession," if true, could have been many things other than the silly braggadocio that it is portrayed as: mere exaggerated "locker-room talk;" intimidating Aquash to make her believe she was dealing with a killer; or some other similar deceit.

Since the 1990s, other prominent Indian voices have ramped up the intensity of the Peltier and Aquash controversies. Journalist Paul DeMain has run a newspaper called *News from Indian Country*,[172] taking editorial shots against AIM to the point where Peltier sued him and demanded DeMain make a public statement as a form of apology.[173] Other writers such as Ward Churchill strenuously support AIM and other Indian issues, although Churchill often finds his comments dismissed by the mainstream press as an unreliable radical.[174]

There is reason to believe that the FBI has always exaggerated the tactics of AIM as a brutal terrorist group, spreading rumors throughout the trials of Butler, Robideau, and Peltier that AIM had been planning to bomb the courthouse or kill the jurors. In fact, Trimbach quotes a section from Means's autobiography where Means claims that at his own trial, he was going to shoot everyone in the courtroom should the jury find him guilty.[175] Although there is no evidence that AIM was planning anything violent during any court proceedings, especially in the case against Butler and Robideau in which the AIM members actually won, AIM did have the capacity to intimidate others in their ranks who betrayed their cause.

For example, the situation with Norman Brown, a Navajo who was in Tent City with Peltier, Butler, Robideau and others, illustrates how the intimidation and deception went both ways—first from the FBI, then from AIM. At first, he was to be a witness for the prosecution, although now he claims his planned testimony was coerced:

> "They kept coming to a point where 'who killed the agents. We know you know who killed them. We know you saw Leonard, Bob, and Dino.' And they kept going on and on and they kept reminding me I was going to jail, that I had two counts of first degree murder against me. So, being there by myself, no choice. I sort of went along with them, you know, and it's wrong because it wasn't true."[176]

Clearly any FBI interrogators would be highly trained and skilled at putting on the type of pressure required to get a guilty person to crack. On the other hand, as was the case with Myrtle Poor Bear, in the heat of the situation, these professional tactics could quickly become an inducement to lie, as Brown claimed later:

> "They handcuffed me and that's when they threatened my mother. They said, 'you know, you little, you little, shit and … you may never see your mother again.' That's when it really hit me."[177]

While the FBI agents all flatly deny such claims, Trimbach points to AIM tactics of intimidation, which Brown also acknowledges, but on a much smaller scale of public shaming:

> "They marched me in and this whole crowd of Native people. As I was walking down the aisle there, I heard words spoken to me, 'there's that sellout,' 'there's that pig,' and 'there's that little asshole—that's him, hey asshole!' It was like a little whisper."[178]

Still, of all the reasons for AIM to use deception and intimidation, the most strange and bizarre public relations breakdown amidst all these rumors and lack of reliable journalism involved William Janklow, whose sensational antics of speeding through the back roads of South Dakota, drunk and without wearing pants, culminated after several arrests and convictions in his actually hitting and killing a motorcyclist.[179] Janklow was also a litigant against Matthiessen for defamation,[180] and was a suspect in the murder of Jancita Eagle Dear (1952-1975), a teenaged Indian girl of some prominence in the AIM saga, who accused Janklow of raping her.[181] As one of the original prosecutors of Peltier, he exhibited a different zeal as he waged a campaign of appeals against his otherwise open-and-shut involuntary manslaughter conviction, but the most interesting aspect is that in an era of scandal mongering, the mainstream press almost completely sat on the Janklow story.

3. Summing Up the Peltier Facts

Between the extremes of deception on the part of both the FBI and AIM, certain overlooked facts help put together a more complete picture of what might have happened on June 26, 1975, when Agents Coler and Williams were tragically killed. Both the Matthiessen and Trimbach books have facts in them that support a more complete picture.

First of all and foremost, it should always be mentioned that the day before the shootout occurred, Richard Wilson had just signed a deal to turn over 100,000 acres of the Pine Ridge Reservation (known as "the Stronghold Unit") to the U.S. Government.[182] This was land that during World War II had been used for military target practice, but the ultimate purpose of Wilson's transfer remains unknown. Although questions of legality have been raised as to Wilson's legitimate power to make such a transfer, there must have been some trepidation on the part of the FBI that some sort of protest or demonstration by AIM might occur.

Trimbach points out that Agents Coler and Williams had visited the Jumping Bull Compound the night before the shootout and was familiar with the area.[183] Therefore, if the agents were chasing a red pickup or some other vehicle onto Jumping Bull Compound, they would have the scene fresh in their minds.

Another important detail is that an 18-year-old Robert Ecoffey, who went on to join the FBI and lead the investigation into the Aquash murder,[184] was a BIA Police intern who was with Coler and Williams the morning they were killed and exchanged information with them. Coler was not as familiar with the situation, because he was originally stationed in Denver.[185]

A very important detail that Matthiessen glosses over is that one of the items found in Coler's car after the shootout was a detailed map of the Jumping Bull Compound, with indications as to where bunkers filled with weapons might be located.[186] This is not only further proof that the agents had been studying this area, but they knew, as was indeed the case, that AIM was stockpiling weapons there.[187] If a cover story about the cowboy boot theft was protecting the real purpose of the agents for being in Jumping Bull Compound that day, the real purpose might have been simply to gather intelligence about the AIM camp and the types and numbers of weapons they might have collected there.

According to the information gathered from an eye witness at the Compound, Angie Long Visitor, about the AIM camp, or Tent City, seven men and three women (ten in all) would have been there when the shootout took place: Bob Robideau, Norman Brown, Leonard Peltier, Mike Anderson, Wish Draper, Norman Charles, Jean Bordeaux, Lena "Lynn" Gunston, and Nilak Butler.[188] Peltier's actual girlfriend (not Myrtle Poor Bear, but Norma Jean Croy) had earlier been at Tent City as well, but not on the day of the shootout.[189]

Long Visitor lived in a small green shack on the compound with her husband Ivis and three children. She heard the shots and looked out her window, seeing the two cars which the agents were shooting from, and one of the agents shooting in her direction, southeast, at an angle that was more easterly than where Tent City was located behind a group of trees.[190] In an FBI report, she also claimed she heard shots coming from the trees to the left (west) of the cars.[191] The FBI report goes on to say as Long Visitor was making her escape, she noticed Peltier's Chevrolet van in the area next to the agents' cars, but does not mention Peltier was there, although she recognized Bob Robideau, Norman Charles, and Joe Stuntz shooting at the agents.[192]

Furthermore, Norman Brown says that he and Joe Stuntz heard the shots and ran up unarmed from Tent City to investigate.[193] When they discerned that shooting was occurring in the Jumping Bull Compound, although were unable to see anything or discern who was shooting or at what, the two teenagers ran back to Tent City to report to the older AIM members that a firefight was underway, got their guns, and returned to the scene.[194] Butler had been sleeping when he heard the two teenagers tell him there was shooting. Peltier claims he too was in the Tent City when the shooting began:

> "When I heard the shooting I ran up to the Jumping Bull house, and
> I seen that there was police cars bound by the highway already."[195]

Brown also says he saw Peltier shooting from the area where several junked cars were located, more in the vicinity of Tent City.[196] Brown also remembers when the BIA Police car arrived, around the same time as Gary Adams' car, apparently shortly before Agents Coler and Williams were executed, and describes how he was perfectly capable of killing one of the drivers if he wanted to:

> "I had him in my sights you know, like I had the figure of his head, basically I was aiming right at him, you know. But I couldn't do that, I couldn't shoot him. So I shot his front tire out."[197]

Trimbach makes much of the issue that Peltier's van was the only vehicle on the compound that was operable, but that certainly does not mean that others were not permitted to drive it.[198] The AIM defense depends on their claim that there were many other Indians on the Jumping Bull Compound that day, and that someone other than the AIM members, who admit to participating in the firefight, delivered the crucial coup de grâce shots that killed the agents. Trimbach attempts to poke further holes in Long Visitor's account, claiming she should have recognized the "strange cars" of the agents, because they had visited the property the day before, even though there is no known record of her encountering or seeing these cars the day before.[199] Referring to her facetiously as "eagle-eyed Angie,"[200] Trimbach continues an attempt to impeach her account of what she saw in one part of Matthiessen's book,[201] claiming she should have seen Peltier and others to the left of her but did not mention this, although in the FBI report of Long Visitor's account, which Matthiessen includes in another part of his book,[202] she does see AIM members shooting to her left, but only Robideau, Charles, and Stuntz, and doesn't mention she saw Peltier.[203]

Bob Robideau admits that he fired the shot that injured Agent Coler's arm, as well as the shot that injured Williams ("I had discovered that they both had been hit by my gunfire"[204]). Certainly Robideau in his own words appears to have been closer to the situation than either Peltier or Butler:

> "We needed to capture these two agents. We didn't know that they were agents at the time. We didn't have any idea who they were. But we felt it had become necessary to, ah, to, ah, capture them. And that's what we were going to do. And we cautiously started to make our way towards these two cars, and about half way, I heard several shots fired ...

27

> When we arrived at the cars, we discovered that both these indi-
> viduals were dead. At that   moment, it seemed, our whole lives had
> been transformed. There was nothing left. The only thing we could
> look forward to, ah, was death. And at that moment we knew it."[205]

Of course if Robideau had been willing to lie about the Mr. X story, his version of the shooting could also be suspect. Then again, if he was the one who delivered the coup de grâce shots to the agents, he could have in theory gotten away with confessing after his trial, since the "not guilty" verdict would have given him protection against double jeopardy. That verdict was the result of an affirmative defense of self-defense, which means the jury determined that he did the act of double homicide, but had legal justification to do it. Of course, Butler's verdict was in essence the same as Robideau's, even though he was in a completely different position during the event.

Although he did not show up to testify at the trial of Butler and Robideau, Mike Anderson had made the now discredited statement that Jimmy Eagle and his girlfriend Wilma had been at Tent City. Anderson further testified at Peltier's trial that he had been conveniently situated on the roof of the home of Wanda Siers in the Compound, giving him a view of the entire scene, and saw Peltier come out of his Chevrolet van and begin the firefight. Norman Brown now says that Anderson was in Tent City at that time ("No, he was down there with us. He was with us before the shooting happened."[206]), as did Jean Bordeaux, one of the women in Tent City at the time ("He was around the camp. I think he was changing clothes or hanging clothes up, or airing something out, but he was like busy around the tent, you know."[207]).

Most damaging to Peltier's case was the ballistics report linking a shell casing found in the trunk of one of the agents' cars to his AR-15.[208] Judge Gerald Heaney explains that even though the Government improperly withheld a previous ballistics report that had excluded Peltier's AR-15 as matching the shell casing, this did not meet the standard of probability[209] that a jury would have come to a different verdict in order to grant Peltier a new trial:

> "The standard that the Supreme Court has established for granting
> a new trial is that you have to be convinced that it was reasonably
> probable that the jury would have reached an opposite result had
> the new evidence been presented to them. Now that's a high stan-
> dard. If the standard was one of possibility rather than probability
> we would have reached a different result."[210]

Even if Heaney's conjectural assessment of the probability standard for granting a new trial is reasonable in regard to what a jury would likely make of these two contradictory ballistics tests, which appears to exclude the possibility of a jury also considering Heaney's own assessment that the FBI acted improperly by withholding the first of these tests, it's easy to succumb to a feeling that the justice system has failed.

When any jury is seated in a court within the United States, how many of these peers of the defendant generally understand that the FBI has been known to aggressively pursue their version of the case, even if it requires falsely making up evidence? Judge Heaney constructs an ideal abstraction that carefully but thoroughly scrubs away any notion of corruption, since the court that includes the bench he is sitting on is ultimately just as much a part of the corruption as anything the FBI did to manufacture evidence.

All things considered, if the evidence employed by the Government's general dealing with Peltier beginning with his extradition from Canada appeared to be based on information the FBI ultimately made up out of whole cloth (Poor Bear affidavits, Mike Anderson testimony that he was on a roof and could see Peltier get out of his van, Jimmy Eagle's presence at Tent City, and the improperly withheld ballistics test), clemency for Peltier does seem an appropriate remedy. Of course, the FBI through the voice of Trimbach and others will find every way to argue that their methods are sound (even if they clearly were not), and AIM members supporting Peltier will continue to push for clemency challenging the justice Judge Heaney and others have ruled upon under the circumstances. In the end, clemency is certainly appropriate when there is a mess made of things through either mistakes, impropriety or both.

Finally, in one last example of the way in which certain facts in this case are distorted and have no resolution, Peltier lawyer William Kunstler describes the way in which Agent Gary Adams is on record as describing a red vehicle leaving the compound less than a half hour after the agents were killed, but then denies the record could be correct:

> "When we had him on the stand in Cedar Rapids, Gary Adams denied that he ever said that. He denied it and said that it might have been a mistake, that maybe the stenographer got it wrong or what have you. But that it simply wasn't true."[211]

Of course, if the record were indeed correct, it would indicate that the agents probably did chase a red vehicle, not Peltier's van, onto the compound and that it fled the scene afterwards, leaving a very viable suspect for the shooting unknown and at large. Peltier's van never left the scene. Whoever this was has not yet stepped forward or been definitively identified. Still, keep in mind that Kunstler is a scrappy and aggressive defense attorney in this case and the story about a red vehicle was eventually denied by Butler.

4. Summing up the Aquash Facts

When Aquash's murder remained a mystery in the eyes of those curious enough to entertain theories about it, the lion's share of these theories reasonably pointed to Dick Wilson and GOONs as suspects. Some even suggested assistance by the FBI in at least disrupting the chain of evidence and investigation.[212] These same theorists suffered disorienting whiplash during the 180-degree turnabout in which the FBI commenced a zealous investigation making prime suspects out of members of AIM.

The theory that produced two convictions in court that certain AIM members executed Aquash for being a snitch indeed must have created utter shock and confusion among researchers of the Peltier case and related events. Aquash's murder never became as notorious or famous as the case against Peltier, but many who always smelled something fishy about the circumstances surrounding Aquash's murder may have been too stunned to delve deeply into the FBI's new evidence. Clearly, the FBI's timing and boldness effectively carried with it an element of shock and awe.

Russell Means, for example, criticized the fact that only two "foot soldiers" were ultimately convicted. They really had no personal motive to kill Aquash other than following orders in an organization they wanted to be in.

Still, the original FBI scenario had Aquash being driven to the home of Means's brother (Bill Means) before her execution on the highway.[213] Means therefore followed these two trials carefully but never expressed any assertive doubt about the veracity of the FBI's evidence and theory of the FBI's cases against Looking Cloud and Graham.

Other prominent AIM leaders, such as John Trudell, publically acknowledged his understanding of the new facts without making any claims they were false. Dennis Banks, who had called Aquash the love of his life, also never accused the FBI of inventing a case to further discredit Peltier or to cover up some still unknown motive that would have led to Aquash's death. Both Trudell and Banks were prominent members of AIM, which begs the question as to how the ranks of AIM were ultimately organized and why a death sentence against one of its members apparently eluded prominent members who worked closely and had strong personal bonds of friendship with that condemned member.

If the FBI acted improperly preparing the evidence for the Peltier case, much of the motivation came from the way Robideau and Butler were acquitted on a self-defense theory, when Agent Williams's death occurred while he was presumably trying to surrender before being ignobly executed, and Coler's occurred while he was minutes if not seconds away from dying anyway. If the FBI were improperly building the case against Graham and Looking Cloud, the motive for doing so had not nearly the immediacy and strong emotions as Peltier's case did. Still, the ongoing FBI campaign against clemency for Peltier makes the emergence of the case against Graham and Looking Cloud a convenient way to keep its cause going.

Still, Looking Cloud remains the primary source for much of the new information in the Aquash murder case, and the way the FBI interrogated him is a matter of record. As a heroin addict tormented with a guilty conscience for being a participant in a homicide, Looking Cloud relied on his "blood brother," a friend named Richard Two Elk, to coax out the demons in his memory. Looking Cloud's confession almost became a form of therapy, with Two Elk and the FBI assuring him that he'll "feel better" once he has confessed all of the details of his bad deed.

In this way, nothing about Looking Cloud's fate in the American justice system suggests he made any sort of high pressure deal in exchange for information crucial to the FBI's case. It was all freely provided. More likely, the coaxers of this confession were more interested in building a criminal case against Looking Cloud than nurturing his well-being and state of mind.

One of the taped confessions posted online also reveals details that were not only coaxed out of Looking Cloud but repeatedly insisted upon even though repeatedly denied by Looking Cloud, such as the incident involving driving Aquash to the house of Bill Means that night.

Meanwhile, Graham has always denied the FBI's case against him. His denial would have been legally much stronger if he simply denied ever driving Aquash anywhere. By admitting that he did once drive Aquash to Pine Ridge Indian Reservation within the timeframe of the FBI scenario, he freely stipulates part of the prosecution's case against him—it places him in the car with her. All legal machinations aside, Graham's version of events would have us believe that Aquash was transported from Colorado to South Dakota safely and was dropped off alone. If Graham is telling

31

the truth, that would mean the woman eyewitnesses saw loaded into the Pinto hatchback tied to a board must have been someone else.

The most implausible part of the FBI's story involves the way the coroner declared exposure as the cause of the Jane Doe's death. Ample blood on her clothes, and hair found on the side of the cliff indicating at least trauma to her head as she fell clearly suggest something other than exposure. Other cases of exposure during a harsh winter on the Pine Ridge Indian Reservation may involve people wandering into the wilderness in a drunken state, but this Jane Doe was located too far away from any populated area. Someone else must have transported her there and abandoned her.

The fact that the Jane Doe's body must have been buried in snow for two months would have possibly obscured her features enough to be unrecognizable. It may also account for the way the hands of the Jane Doe had to be removed and probably rehydrated before providing fingerprints.

What has been practically the battle cry for DeMain's journalistic efforts to bring justice for Aquash's murder involve the incident that when Peltier was asked to vet Aquash at a Farmington, New Mexico AIM Convention, he threatened her by putting a gun in her mouth.[214] In many ways, one wonders about the activities of two militant revolutionaries when one challenges the other's loyalty. Peltier has commented on this incident, and Matthiessen mentions it in his book as Peltier and Aquash goofing around.[215] Of course if Peltier is lying about the mood of the incident, resorting to the "we were just kidding" defense is a bit farfetched. On the other hand, Aquash defiantly scolded Peltier that day, daring him to go ahead and shoot her if he really suspected her of being an informant.[216]

Ultimately, the most important fact that emerges from this meeting between Peltier and Aquash is that she was defiant, even feisty, to the end. This included her irrepressible attitude towards other AIM members, especially those in the ruling elite and authority of AIM, let alone towards the FBI and police.[217]

This demonstration of Aquash's disposition accomplishes at least two things: it dispels DeMain's sensationalism, because she was not someone that would allow herself to be a helpless victim to police or let herself be victimized by other AIM members; and it also raises the question as to how and why she would ever finally let herself be "arrested" or "detained" by Theda Clarke in order to face accusations by the AIM members that she was an informant. There are simply not enough facts about Clarke to explain why she, more than an imposing warrior like Peltier, would have the power to detain Aquash in the basement, when Aqaush had no qualms about fleeing the American justice system as a fugitive, or standing up to any of Peltier's taunts. In fact, Graham's claim that things were indeed "heating up" at Yellow Wood's home with Clarke to the point where Aquash called him so she could get out of there is more consistent with Aquash's overall character.[218]

In light of this, even if Aquash did submit to the authority that Clarke supposedly asserted over her, would this still be considered a kidnapping? Even all the other rumors involving Clarke tying Aquash to a board and stuffing her into the back of a Pinto hatchback appear to be things Aquash did not resist—if true. This makes the theory that the witnesses who testified that they saw all this might have seen someone else they thought was Aquash.

Meanwhile the small inconsistencies in this tale of a midnight kidnapping and execution stubbornly remain: a Pinto hatchback has a large window that would allow any motorist to see into it, making it risky indeed to tie up Aquash and put her back there; if Looking Cloud indeed fired the remaining rounds in the pistol into the ground, why were no extra bullets recovered at the murder scene after a thorough search of the area; and why is it that Candy Hamilton testified that she saw Aquash at the AIM meeting that was purportedly serving as her death trial, but there was no mention of Clarke, Looking Cloud or Graham being at that meeting. Graham's theory that the meeting with Hamilton's sighting actually took place after the Government's theory of Aquash's death date was never allowed into Graham's trial.[219]

If anything, a substantial question remains in that if AIM members were indeed involved in Aquash's death, this does not put to rest other controversies, let alone shut the door on Peltier's case for executive clemency. Other problems include what happens when trying to solve a murder decades after it was committed; using its facts for another purpose of derailing someone else's bid for executive clemency; using the case built by an FBI investigator who was closely associated with the victims of Peltier's crime; using a strong-willed FBI associate to become the "blood brother" of a heroin addict whose loose lips would eventually sink his own version of the story, which was that he was an innocent bystander; and in light of a string of fraudulently manufactured evidence in Peltier's case, why would we not suspect that such tactics were also employed to amass the cases against Looking Cloud and Graham?

Unfortunately as time goes by, and Peltier gets closer to dying in prison, those with stubborn suspicions about these legal dealings and their ramifications become fewer. The tug-of-war between letting Aquash finally rest in peace and justice for Peltier now shows the former as the prevailing sentiment.

FOCAL POINT THREE: POSTMODERN AFTER-THOUGHT

If "[p]ostmodernism refers to a congeries of theoretical supposition about the nature of language,"[220] and it can also be applied to law,[221] applying it to a congeries of facts may provide a more complete picture of this Aquash puzzle which, despite its boasts, the justice system provides only an illusion of solving. Certainly, all the other victims of the "Reign of Terror"[222] still do not have such carefully litigated and publicized justice. If postmodern analysis of law has employed tireless scholars who artfully debunk the notion of a universal "Rule of Law,"[223] and if postmodernism is applied to the often skewed logic of Federal Indian law, especially in otherwise contradictory legal doctrines set forth in the Indian Child Welfare Act[224] and the notorious dodging of racial issues in *Morton v. Mancari*,[225] how further can postmodernism tolerate rights to preserve the identity of groups?[226] Would postmodernism dare tolerate as a local sovereign matter, say, an Indian tribal government that declares martial law?

Meanwhile, criminal liability beyond two Indian foot soldiers acting upon orders from "higher-ups" in AIM or even the FBI (which actually had profound influence over the upper levels of AIM[227]) now ends in vows of silence and rumors of snitch-jacketing.[228] Still, a postmodern or inconclusive amalgamation of the facts remains the most complete and appropriate picture of what happened if all that remains are legal judgments that do not entirely make sense, challenged typically by myriad independent theories.[229]

Meanwhile, the final piece of the puzzle remains "the Stronghold" or "South Unit," which for reasons unknown, was conveyed to the National Park Service. This land has been reported to have everything from human remains to uranium deposits to black-op helicopters hidden on it.[230]

Any implementation of a modern legal system involves voluminous texts, written down officially, printed in journals and newspapers, published on the Internet, and even spread purely by word of mouth. This system must come to grips with its own inability in the modern world to stand as a respected institution based solely on the immediate meaning of these texts.

CHAPTER TWO

APPLIED LEGAL HERMENEUTICS

This chapter is divided into five parts as follows: the first part explores how American common law has always had its own notion of "legal hermeneutics"; the second part introduces the elusive "nuts and bolts" of the approach to hermeneutics since the Enlightenment and how the term "phronesis" has become an important handle[231]; the third part further explores the Enlightenment as perhaps the source of spinning the idea of interpretation into the current issue between originalism and legal hermeneutics; the fourth part uses a specific example from Justice Scalia's interpretation of the Eighth Amendment demonstrating how the two sides of this issue clash; and finally, the fifth part shows how the hermeneutics of suspicion have brought out some more controversy about the ongoing debate about hermeneutics, but ultimately reined it in at the same time, showing as well that Justice Scalia argues just as much from suspicion as the legal hermeneuts do.

AMERICAN COMMON LAW

If the articulation "legal hermeneutics" were a purely philosophical invention, a jurist might attempt to argue that it has no place in the practicing legal world whatsoever.[232] In other words, whatever philosophers think of lawyers might be valuable observations among philosophers themselves or even to laypeople interested in philosophy, if not only marginally to lawyers themselves, but has nothing reliably useful to offer jurists that would be authoritative, aside from informal constructive criticism. After all, lawyers require specialized training that philosophers typically do not undergo. In essence, lawyers are also the only ones required by society to set the standard as to how to understand their own sort of insider lingual acrobatics, such as those appearing in legal opinions, statutes, and legal memos, even though clearly lawyers must embrace publically the premise that their ideas are packed into such carefully simplified language, the average citizen can understand them.

As a matter of consistency, a garden variety lawyer locked inside their own concept of what the legal world is may even apply their own version of a doctrine of *stare decisis* (which actually has been a hermeneutical rule all along, as demonstrated *infra*[233]): outside interdisciplinary ideas of legal hermeneutics should only be relevant to common law if a judge somewhere in a high court applied them to an actual decision. The equally common philosopher might take the bait to this argument by quibbling that all uses of language fall under the purview of modern philosophy, including even the most extreme or esoteric legalese, and, as long as lawyers, legislators, and judges are using language, they must yield authority over cutting edge developments of philosophy which sheds light on any new discoveries concerning the mysteries of meaning and interpretation. As kneejerk sensibilities, both approaches will help very little to penetrate Gadamer's approach to interpreting legal texts, but find their way nonetheless into the often cruel battlefield that is the modern practice of American law.

If necessary, these ultimately quixotic arguments could be bypassed thanks to Francis Lieber (1800-1872),[234] whose early 19th-century notion of legal hermeneutics actually was introduced into New York case law.[235] Moreover, Lieber's three-part classification of his approach to legal hermeneutics amounts to essentially the way law is still actually practiced and interpreted today: 1) variations of today's Rules of Construction, which lawyers are supposed to learn often with Latin mottos such as "in pari materia" and which have been quoted in Latin in hundreds of American cases[236]; 2) using precedents, which is a general concept that supports the doctrine of *stare decisis* itself; and 3) authorities, which finds itself in today's discussion of law in the form of articles and various writings and records of legislators, but also in the use of Restatements, which of course are not considered law, but are often used in legal opinions to interpret statutes and cases. In fact, Lieber's very important distinction between interpretation and construction, which occurs within the first of his three categories of hermeneutics, emphasizes that interpretation has always sought to find the original intent of the lawmaker, while construction gives the interpreter license to actually build extra unstated rules into a law where necessary.

After Lieber's rudimentary concept of legal hermeneutics found its way into New York courts and common law, it created progeny there well into the 20th-century,[237] as well as scattering to other mostly southern states,[238] especially making a strong showing in the Supreme Court of

Missouri.[239] These references generally treat legal hermeneutics reverently, as if the topic had been incorporated into American common law, and that Lieber's work should be almost common knowledge to any competent lawyer.

The notable exception to this reverence was California, which in the first half of the 20th-century produced a string of criminal law opinions that consistently used "legal hermeneutics" with the utmost skepticism, even sarcasm, without explanation. The California rule thus even permanently combined the articulation "legal hermeneutics" with the word "legerdemain" as a way of dismissing any argument that on its face appears to be too wordy, convoluted, or without common sense.[240]

When comparing these cases from New York with those of California, the only common ground shared between them is that the articulation "legal hermeneutics" without even defining it invokes strong passions. For those courts that supported Lieber's notions, legal hermeneutics is a sophisticatedly philosophically honed mechanism which can act as a referee whenever a dispute over the meaning of a legal text might lead to uncertain application. For the California courts, legal hermeneutics needs no other explanation other than it is a deliberately intimidating and beguiling way of avoiding the truth of the matter.

Still, without some affirmation or mention from the courts that distinguishes what sort of legal hermeneutics is referred to, more ambiguity can be formed. Because all three branches of Lieber's approach (i.e, Rules of Construction, precedents, and authorities) are now widely accepted, and the dismissive and sarcastic tone of California criminal courts became generally the stance Neo-Conservatives take,[241] any mention today of legal hermeneutics could be referring to either of these extremes, although rarely to something else.

For stubborn skeptics who might still complain that Continental intellectualism has no place in American law, Lieber's brief and unorthodox German education at the University of Jena suggests that he must have had access to Continental hermeneutics and German philosophy as they existed in the early 19th-century before bringing these ideas in an important way to America. Thankfully, Gadamer's *Truth and Method* also finally finds its way into the courts, if not entirely obliquely.[242]

In *Stupak-Thrall v. United States*,[243] a deadlocked, seven-to-seven en banc Court of Appeals in the Sixth Circuit argued about the meaning of the phrase "subject to valid existing rights" as it applied to Forest Service regulations promulgated from the Michigan Wilderness Act of 1997.[244] In light of the tie vote and high passions on both sides of the argument, the impasse ultimately meant the lower court was technically "affirmed" as if no appeal had taken place at all. The court nevertheless memorialized its grandiose non-decision with two vociferously opposing opinions.

Judge Karen Nelson Moore (b. 1948), a Clinton appointee, defends the regulations in question which would make rules for sail boats and house boats on even small remote lakes, including one central to the litigation in the upper peninsula of Michigan.[245] Judge Danny Julian Boggs (b. 1944), a Reagan appointee, sides with dwellers near the lake who have claimed the rules were interfering with their riparian rights.

In a very typical left-right political exchange out of the still young post-Reagan era, Boggs presents a much lengthier opinion (34 pages) than Moore's (a little more than 3 pages), while simultaneously claiming the case is actually a "very simple" case.[246] Towards the end of the opinion, Boggs delivers his version of a coup de grâce by citing five articles in a footnote which he claims are dedicated to the ambiguity in the Constitution concerning whether the President should be 35 years of age (even though only the first article facetiously examines this[247]).

Boggs's strategy here follows the California criminal courts' approach to legal hermeneutics: rolling one's eyes and pretending that some malicious element has infected the otherwise healthy body of law. By making a broadside attack on "critical legal studies," even chiding law review commentaries in general based on Moore's precise mention of a 375-page study by the University of Kentucky studying the ambiguous meaning of "subject to valid existing rights," Boggs appeals to a populism by citing a survey of articles he probably has not even read.

Fortunately, among these articles is a seminal article by Mootz about Gadamer's legal hermeneutics.[248] Although this is no red carpet for Gadamer's legal hermeneutics to make a grand entrance into American case law on, and Boggs is fraily attempting humor, embellishing the sarcasm of the California criminal courts, it indirectly introduces hermeneutics into American common law as commentary.

THE ELUSIVE "NUTS AND BOLTS" OF MODERN HERMENEUTICS

What Lieber's name suggests in so many New York legal opinions is that basic rules of legal hermeneutics have existed in American law from an early date and are preserved in many of its common law doctrines. Despite this fact, a practicing jurist is still not necessarily compelled to make the connection between Lieber and, say, the cliché of a lawyer quoting a Latin motto when addressing an issue as to how a statute should be interpreted and, in doing so, seeming to end any debate of the statute's true meaning with the same certainty of the inanimate nature of the dead language employed. Perhaps the certainty of dead language gives an interpreter more confidence, and if the text itself is declared dead, it is more predictable than a "living" text in which meanings change over time.

Whether or not the interpretation of a law might stretch outside of a common application of how it might otherwise have been used up to that point in time, the legal hermeneutics rubric serves as simply a reminder that there is nothing licentious or improper about interpreting or constructing upon a preexisting law in a way that has never been tried before. Just the same, the open-minded jurist of today who recognizes something useful about Gadamerian legal hermeneutics ought to beware of the mocking accusations of those like Judge Boggs. This includes the impatient hope that simply mentioning Lieber's name, let alone Gadamer's, is all one needs to know in order to start snipping and amending statutes and making sweeping declarations that are supposed to be based on the legal ideas stated within the four corners of a legal opinion. After all, Lieber was able to codify his ideas into a handy list that can be followed step-by-step without much extra explanation.[249]

On the other hand, what Gadamer represents is no such pat and simple do-it-yourself manual to interpretation, rather, the result of centuries of German transcendental philosophy combining pregnant concepts mostly out of Classical Antiquity with a freely intuitive "play" (Spiel[250]) between understanding and interpretation. With that given as the purpose of the "machinery," the "nuts and bolts" of it are too numerous, difficult to find, and even often difficult to determine to think of hermeneutics as anything so scientifically based as a machine.

Compared with the likes of Lieber as a seeming relic of the 19th-century to build on in American law, Gadamer espouses a much larger, expansive picture for legal hermeneutics as to what should be recognized about how language is used generally, as well as specifically in the law, even though this picture basically depicts what has already been commonly practiced. As such, legal hermeneutics consists of a collection of indispensable rules in the form of rehashing ancient concepts for the interpretation of legal language. In America, this has been used to defend interpretations of the Constitution, other legal interpretations in the form of legal opinions, and interpreting duly enacted statutes.

Gadamer states explicitly that legal hermeneutics relies on Aristotelian concepts, but especially phronesis, as developed by his mentor Martin Heidegger (1889-1976),[251] not to mention as developed by Heidegger and others in contemplation of other historical turning points of Modern Western philosophy, especially the ongoing influence of the *cogito, ergo sum* argument of René Descartes (1596-1650)[252] and Immanuel Kant's (1724-1804) transcendental exploration of how individuals make judgments in general.[253]

Above all, Gadamer stresses how phronesis involves a decision-making process that is starkly distinct from getting universal results out of scientific methodology, which draws its conclusions based on what Aristotle referred to as episteme (Εεπίστημη)[254]: as long as the rules can consistently describe phenomena without exceptions, they may conveniently stand as scientific maxims. While episteme in this way distinguishes itself by deriving scientific knowledge based on the combination of inductive reasoning and demonstration, phronesis distinguishes itself in two ways distinct from scientific knowledge: 1) it provides another type of certainty based on inductive reasoning and demonstration, but not necessarily in describing physical phenomena, but in human behavior based on preferring reason to base instincts; and 2) it also does not steer itself by searching for something universal, rather, it stresses the individual's perception of specific instances.[255] The stressing of the individual within its specificity and indispensability within phronesis has proved an important, but also controversial aspect, when the process ostensibly attempts to do without the individual.[256]

The process of forming judgments involving phronesis also distinguishes itself from nous (νοῦς, which is Latinized as intellectus), which involves reason and the ability to determine what is true. Both phronesis and nous involve the dianoetic (διανοεῖν) process, which develops a step-by-step method of cognition or argumentation with an often unforeseen outcome, but based on rationality (ratio) and understanding.[257] In its purest form with nous, the dianoetic process resembles the proofs of geometry (mos geometricus) and its certainty. The more immediate noetic (νοεῖν) process makes pre-judgments based on first impressions and intuition,[258] or, as Gadamer writes extensively about in terms of Heidegger's "pre-judgment" structure (Vorurteile),[259] the immediate notion that our senses pick up on that does not yet require a judgment.[260]

Reflecting on this now more sophisticated process of cognition and the several steps it takes before getting to understanding, let alone interpretation, Aristotle has described phronesis as the "eye of the soul," (ὅμμα τῆς ψυχῆς),[261] concluding that because it may or may not involve following a set pattern of rules, it also has a noetic element to it.[262] In other words, common sense can still be a factor when lacking conclusive data (or scientific knowledge) as to whether a left or right turn in a maze leads you out of the puzzle or not.

The often employed distinctions in translation of Classical Greek into Latin-based languages, specifically the meaning and various applications of the word "phronesis" in Aristotle's conception of practical philosophy (πρᾶχις), as compared to the words "techne" (τέχνη) and "sophia" (σοφία), reveals a thread that runs through much of modern legal hermeneutics. To illustrate this with a specific example, "phronesis" has been commonly Latinized as "prudentia," which in American law often helps distinguish a merely "reasonable person" (based purely on νοῦς or intellectus) standard with that of a "reasonably prudent person." The other Greek concepts fall into more familiar modern language forms: "techne" is often associated with "technique," while "sophia" usually means "wisdom" (i.e., divine wisdom as opposed to practical wisdom), despite varied and numerous other uses of its original form.

Once this prudence can be distinguished from wisdom, technique, episteme or nous, the source of Gadamer's distinction between legal hermeneutics and a more general philosophical hermeneutics lies deep within the philosophies of Heidegger. Playing dramatically off of Descartes's *cogito* as the essence of modern ontology, Heidegger substitutes Decartes's generic form of being in "sum" (I am) with a more nuanced form of being in "Da-sein" (which Heidegger stresses as a compound word of the two German words for "there" and "to be").[263] Heidegger then reminds us that ontology or the study of the nature of being has always been accomplished in past philosophy without the consideration of time.[264] Adding the time dimension alters ontology into a more appropriate model of the 20th-century universe.

Heidegger further develops Da-sein in many cryptic ways, often coining his own German words, compounds and usages, but eventually arrives at one crucial point at the notion that Da-sein is understanding in and of itself.[265] Heidegger's further development of the notion of "facticity" (Faktizität)[266] as something deeply related to Aristotle's and even Augustine's notion of "anima,"[267] supporting this notion of Da-sein as "being thrown" (Geworfenheit)[268] as opposed to a stable existence (Vorhanden-heit).[269] The former represents the living element in understanding.

Because Gadamer attempts to unravel as many of Heidegger's cryptic notions to the best of his knowledge and ability, even simplifying them (substituting, for example, the word "being" for Heidegger's "Da-sein"), critics such as Jürgen Habermas[270] and Vattimo[271] have accused him of "urbanizing" Heidegger.[272] On the other hand, Gadamer's status as Heidegger's student brings forth many observations of an insider before Heidegger's *Sein und Zeit* was even published, especially the fact that Gadamer's interest began with Heidegger's lectures on Aristotle's *On the Soul* (*De anima* or Περί Ψυχῆς), early in the 1920s.[273] It should also never be taken lightly that in some influential avenues of literature during the 1920s, various experimental and avant-garde styles at the hands of writers such as James Joyce or even Bertolt Brecht were considered important enough to allow cutting-edge thinkers like Heidegger to experiment with prose in his own way.

In this context, Heidegger made his next step after linking understanding with Da-sein in the connection between understanding and interpretation (Auslegung).[274] Already developed earlier in *Sein und Zeit* is much about the way "circular reasoning" (Zirkel der Beweis)[275] is unavoidable in hermeneutics,[276] but also as something which can become "vicious" (vitiosum)[277] when the step-by-step process of interpretation employs circular reasoning while ascending one level in an attempt to define another. Gadamer transformed this purely cognitive notion by Heidegger into a more social notion of a hermeneutical circle,[278] although Heidegger had already hinted at this more social notion with his trilogy of concepts known as "with-the-world" (Mitwelt), "being-with" (Mitsein), and "with-Da-sein" (Mitdasein).[279]

In order to flesh out hermeneutics further, another elusive concept Heidegger employed occurred in his word for "disclosed" (erschlossen), which according to handwritten notes in the margins of *Sein und Zeit* is associated with the Greek word "ἀλήθεια."[280] One common Latinization of this word is "veritas," which in English is usually "truth," but in Greek also encompasses the Aristotelian notion of "something that reveals itself." In this way, Heidegger's notes also refer to "Lichtung, Licht, Leuchten," which in English would be "lighting, light, to lighten." Although Germans did not have an 18th-century "Enlightenment," at least not with the symbolism of a light turning on or shedding light on something that was once dark, the German "Aufklärung," or an announcement, represented more an important decree upon the politics of the time than shedding light upon the dark Medieval mind and its outmoded conundrums.

There is certainly nothing in free-thinking society that requires anyone to accept Heidegger, Gadamer, or even Aristotle as an immutable or sacred source of Western thought, and it could just as easily be argued that any lost potency in current legal thinking of a notion of phronesis which originated in Antiquity has nothing to do with neglect, but perhaps with a concerted effort to streamline ancient thought into a more efficient use of otherwise abstract theories. In fact, so many of these concepts out of Classical Antiquity tend to be associated with what are now the "occult sciences,"[281] that one tends to assume that these once indispensable philosophical ideas also lack the type of certainty or integrity in methodology required to maintain relevance after the Age of Enlightenment.

Certainly science's efficiency in throwing off once legion rules of how the universe is structured, including the now discarded notion that the world is flat, might consider something like phronesis, with its strong reliance on notions of a soul, to be also not suitable for a worldview now tempered with scientific discipline. Obviously there has been a pronounced clash between science and religion since the Age of Enlightenment drawing a blunt line even among the great religions between accepted doctrine and superstition. Nonetheless, if the Greeks once had even a slightly different grasp on the human capacity to reason and make judgments as compared to what is generally accepted in the practice of law more than two millennia later, there is no reason to ignore this, especially if at least some recent philosophers are heralding a concept like phronesis as something indispensable to interpretation.[282]

On the other hand, the Enlightenment's concern in removing what were now to be declared "pseudo-sciences"—especially pseudo-sciences involving so-called arcane interpretive skills such as phrenology, palmistry, and astrology—out of the recognized and respected canon of knowledge carried with it its own sort of phronesis. The Enlightenment's phronesis helped redefine what people of good moral character (προαίρεσις) were and how such people should support that science was now dictating a more disciplined approach to accepting what was true and what was false.

Now that astronomers only study the arbitrary movement of stars and their purely scientific nature, they would not be distracted from this lofty purpose by also divining "meanings" from them as parts of a Zodiac, influencing the behavior of humans, even though this had been scrupulously "studied" since the Old Babylonian Empire. That the likes of otherwise intelligent people of good moral character (προαίρεσις) like Emanuel Swedenborg and Franz Anton Mesmer could not entirely attain the ideal of this new discipline of the Enlightenment and helped "rediscover" the occult sciences well into the 19th-century, makes for only a slight softening of the otherwise profoundly potent historical and intellectual influence that the Enlightenment had on Western culture.

The problem that arises in this context has an unmistakable irony to it: whether an implied mainstream of thinkers espousing textualism and originalism have somehow similarly discarded concepts such as legal hermeneutics (including Aristotle's phronesis) as if it were mere pseudo-science like astrology and lacked disciplined and rigorous integrity. In this way, the textualists and originalists employ their own unacknowledged form of phronesis to rid the argument of an ancient form of phronesis, all in a simplified but contradictory or even ironic affirmation of tradition.

Obviously Heidegger's philosophical affirmation of even unchartered territory regarding a contemporary application of phronesis, not to mention ontology, resembles in no way the resurrection of what are now occult sciences, because nothing in the post-Enlightenment notion of science suggests that it has anything else to do with the laws of causality and its inductive leap—in other words with Aristotle's notion of episteme, which is distinct from the concept of making decisions based on a mixture of virtue, reason, and morality.[283] In this way, many of the concepts in the practice of law over the centuries have always had a symbiosis with religious and moral concepts, as well as reason. Associating such religious concepts with the purging of pseudo-science that occurred during the Enlightenment proves a baby-with-the-bathwater recklessness, but certainly can be found in some of the tenants of more extreme legal postures such as positivism.[284]

CRISIS IN INTERPRETATION—
THE AGE OF ENLIGHTENMENT

A major challenge of the Enlightenment came in the form of attempting to create for religious intellectualism a new way of reckoning the unscientific nature of many of the Bible's texts—a genuine crisis that had never before been encountered in history, because Western culture's great Holy Book had never before been so upstaged by the accelerating advances of science. Some intellectuals forced themselves to frame the issue as purging out pseudo-science on the one hand, versus blasphemy on the other.

Friedrich Schleiermacher (1768-1834) entered the scene in an effort to find—through an entirely new approach to hermeneutics—a scientific certainty (certitudo sine dubitatione[285]) that once existed in what he perceived to be a traditional interpretation of Biblical texts.[286] Because the newly enhanced blossoming natural sciences of Enlightenment all but challenged the more progressive Protestantism of Schleiermacher's day to find a more progressive way of interpreting Biblical texts,[287] the thrust of Schleiermacher's hermeneutics was primarily theological.

As these methods were later developed and the hermeneutical scope was widened by the likes of Wilhelm Dilthey (1833-1911)[288] to include all of the humanities, especially art, and even later by Heidegger, the word "hermeneutics" became ubiquitous in philosophical works and left the layperson to sort out a trail of historical practices in exegesis, at least since the Enlightenment. A simple dictionary definition of "hermeneutics" as "to interpret" could hardly suffice to explain the usage in works by Heidegger and other philosophers, linguists, and political scientists.

Even though attempts to invent a scientific certainty (such as Schleiermacher's theology or Dilthey's aesthetics) probably partake in extreme examples of crossing the wires of episteme and phronesis that textualism or originalism attempt to do, Schleiermacher and Dilthey's attempts still helped lay the groundwork for Heidegger to shed new light on the divide between episteme and phronesis as well as other aspects of legal hermeneutics.

The fact that the U.S. Constitution was also one of the crown jewels of the Enlightenment movement[289] demonstrates that this era was not only a revolution of strengthening and purifying episteme. The fact that thinkers like Lieber associated his own version of legal hermeneutics with the Enlightenment speaks to the idea that democracy almost by definition requires a sophisticated philosophy of hermeneutics behind it never conceived in monarchies.

Under any rudimentary monarchy systems, a king who both decrees the laws of a nation or tribe and then interprets them as well whenever they were in the king's opinion broken is completely free of any need of hermeneutics, according to its traditional practice. The king thinks he knows what he meant by the decree while decreeing it, and then simply "knows" when someone disobeys his decree, even if the disobedience was something he did not think about when making the decree.

Borrowing from Ricœur's terminology of a text without metaphors as "rhetoric degree zero,"[290] a decree by a king who also enforces his own decree could be a "legal decree degree zero." Such a king's interpretation of his own rule might involve his own private dianoetic process, and maybe this involves his own private phronesis, but if not, the king is free to make any kneejerk reaction to a citizen's "disobedience" at his own pleasure.

When a law is written or decreed by someone not available to explain how it should be enforced, the enforcer must accept the imperfection of not knowing precisely what the king or legislator meant when the law was decreed. When the law is included in a book of laws designated as a holy book, it is much easier to accept that even when interpretation is required of a law, the perfection of a divine author provides the belief in one certain and perfect true meaning that would function perfectly as a law in society were the imperfect humans capable of interpreting it correctly. This has found its way into 20th-century China in the form of Chairman Mao's infamous "Little Red Book."[291]

Certainly America shared deep intellectual sentiments with (along with the language of) England, depicting its newly drafted Constitution in the context of a forward-looking, even quintessential symbolism of the Enlightenment, but finding less influence from France, Germany and other Continental approaches to law—despite the important influences on early America of these countries. The concept of a country without a king actually took the idea of politics in the Enlightenment to its pinnacle with what was then nothing less than a radically new notion of government, even though it was based on an Ancient Greek notion.

While American jurists grew more confident interpreting the laws of their new land instead of the decrees of kings, contemplation about what the legislators were intending with such laws would undoubtedly require contemplation of the intents of everyone who voted for the law, not simply the law's author. Even Justice Scalia criticizes consideration of the legislators' intent, although he generously considers "writings" such as James Madison's *The Federalist* to help explain how the Constitution was understood.[292] Meanwhile, Continental Europe was developing hermeneutics as an approach to interpreting both language and phenomenology itself through a traditional form of philosophy that was at first all but inaccessible to America, but was undoubtedly also aligned with the Enlightenment, albeit in a different way.[293] When considering that extensive approaches to interpreting texts have been examined throughout history, especially in the Pre-Enlightenment world,[294] somehow any new approach to interpretation took on the character in America of something suspicious and foreign, if not an occult science altogether.

Nonetheless, Continental Europe also harbored suspicions about interpreting laws as reflected in several of its burgeoning Civil Codes. Such codes also demonstrate how embellishing laws by further interpreting them somehow goes against a traditional view that recognizes a weakness, if not a mischief, that justifies flouting them.[295] Fundamental Christian notions that there should be no interpretation of the myriad rules of the Bible also famously show how the traditional practice of accepting laws as simple texts that ought not be embellished is a notion that has survived throughout history, even if there might be a naiveté attached to it.

When the original currents of the Enlightenment played out into the full-blown Romanticism of the 19th-century, Kant's concept of the "power of judgment" (Urteilskraft)[296] allowed philosophers to revisit something more concrete, developing further by the 20th-century into a much more expanded notion of hermeneutics, which relied so much on Kant that many in the era called it a "Neo-Kantian" movement. Heidegger borrows from the Neo-Kantians' distinction of a schema for understanding as part of an ongoing understanding of reality and how it plays out in history.[297] More succinctly, this distinction between an ontic and historic reality became an art hidden in the depths of the human soul (verborgene Kunst in den Tiefen der menschlichen Seele).[298]

No matter how carefully written a text is with the purpose of creating a rule that is universal, or at least a rule understandable enough that another person pledged to follow it to the letter cannot possibly make any aberration to its original intent, an interpretation can always be devised that can follow the rule, but run directly opposite to the intention. In this way, writing a law is not unlike confronting any mathematical system for which ultimate perfection is impossible, as is so aptly and popularly depicted in the book *Gödel, Escher, and Bach*.[299]

Originally, the most fundamental rule of legal hermeneutics is what Schleiermacher also believed for theological hermeneutics, that is, that there could only be one "true" interpretation of a text, or universal hermeneutics.[300] Lieber produces several examples of laws deliberately disobeyed according to their original intent but without violating the literal "letter of the law."[301]

Most notably, the Medieval story involving King Conrad III and his royal decree to the women living in the Castle at Weinsberg intended to spare them the slaughter that awaited their husbands by allowing them to leave with whatever personal property they could carry on their backs.[302] The clever women proceeded to exit the castle carrying their husbands on their backs.

To take an example just the opposite of the women of Weinsberg, that is, a law that when meticulously followed tends to directly violate a public policy the law was intended to preserve, Justice Scalia uses the case of *Church of the Holy Trinity v. United States*.[303] In that case, a prominent, historical church in New York City attempted to hire an Englishman to be its rector and pastor, even though a statute forbade American citizens from encouraging aliens to migrate to the United States. Although Scalia admits the statute was probably overbroad and was intended to halt an influx of foreign manual labor into America, which is how the Court in that case justified their decision to allow the Church to hire the Englishman, Scalia also gives this example of a classic case of how the Court got it "wrong and failed to follow the text."[304]

Meanwhile, the modern notions of texualism and originalism[305], which also attempt to debunk modern legal hermeneutics and vice versa, certainly already includes this early notion of "intent of the lawmaker" in it. Whereas originalism deals with interpreting the Constitution, another recent movement of austerity of interpretation known as textualism deals with statutes.

Ultimately, these concepts challenge precariously what Aquinas referred to as "fides informis," or faith without love,[306] because what is implied by the austerity of originalism or textualism is that we must remain emotionally neutral when interpreting law and if the outcome of the interpretation is something that does not please us, the law must still stand without questioning it. This touches again upon the misperception that the only trustworthy text is a dead text. In order to further examine this dispute between texualism and orginalism and legal hermeneutics, it is necessary to further develop the argument, perhaps with an example, since both seemingly rest on a common foundation.

A CRUEL AND UNUSUAL ORIGINALISM

Certainly Justice Antonin Scalia's famous use of both the textualism and orginalism lines of reasoning serves as a good example of not only the Neo-Conservative ideal of jurisprudence, but also, contradictorily, as an active effort at interpretation based on scrupulous use of a rule. But Scalia's rule goes much further than putting into play the tether between what a law tends to mean on its face to a living reader and what that same law was supposed to have meant when it was written by its now dead author(s). In fact, as a textualist interpreter of statutes, he advocates "objectified intent"[307] in a way that not only severs the tether to the living, but to the intent of the dead legislator(s) as well.

With this alone, a neutral observer might expect to observe at least some similarities between Scalia's approach to making rules of interpretation and that of a hermeneut such as Gadamer, because both are involved with divining rules as to how a text is interpreted. On the other hand, Gadamer's approach involves a ubiquitous element of phronesis that allows an interpretation to grow as if it were alive.

At the outset of his philosophy, Scalia declares interpretation a "science,"[308] although distinguishes this process from that of making common law, which is an "art" of distinguishing older cases.[309] He then admits that he only knows of one treatise that explains statutory interpretation as a science.[310]

This approach shares certain sentiments with positivism—or its related philosophies naturalism and logical positivism.[311] It also favors mostly arcane historical research and using it as the source and context of a law—not what the legislator thought the statute meant, let alone what a living reader might think it means.

Like Scalia's textualism, positivism attempts to rid from enforcement of law a sentimentalism that tends to make the rules ultimately too flexible in light of changing norms in the course of history. This flexibility is associated with a sort of laziness[312] which might have mistakenly failed to set a standard in America for statutory interpretation, running the risk of distorting the meaning of a text over time, even since its inception.

Naturalism is similar in this pursuit against alleged laziness in what it perceives to be a lack of discipline in understanding the natural sciences and how once and for all these sciences have toppled the false conundrums of pseudo-science and superstition.[313] The lack of sentiment that positivism can often lead to appears to fuel Naturalism as well.

Meanwhile, hermeneuts also fend off what they might perceive as another sort of laziness in thinkers such as Scalia, Bork, and Berger, in that the ancient traditions of interpreting laws and how laws should be preserved have always involved maintaining a tether between present context and past—even if kings were interpreting their own laws.

Part of the purpose of law—whether ancient or current—is to assuage the violated sentiments of the general public (the so-called retributive purpose). Whether this general public uses the courts for civil disputes, for which litigants expect a just resolution, or becomes entangled as a victim or defendant in criminal cases, for which criminals are expected to be punished appropriately, the law is for their sentiments, not a judge's own ability to fend off sentimentalism.

In this rather ironic way, both textualists and hermeneuts are engaged in extensive analysis of the meanings of words and articulations that appear in legal language. That textualists or positivists might claim they follow an extreme "plain-meaning" interpretation of whatever text might appear as a legal decree, they are still applying rules of construction.

As far as originalism goes, which deals exclusively with interpreting the Constitution, Scalia takes a different tack. Most vividly as opposed to textualism, Scalia's originalism does embrace the premise that modern jurists must take into consideration intent of the legislator(s) and historical context.[314] Scalia denies this consideration is actually reverence to the intent of the legislator, because phrases of the Constitution are still subject to the "objectified intent" of textualism, but admits the Constitution is a broader outline of how to make laws, and therefore requires more historical context as a guide.[315]

It is also important to understand that Scalia admits that in the common law tradition, judges properly created laws to fit the situation, even employing to the word "practical" (a word associated with Aristotle's phronesis) to describe the process.[316] Scalia distinguishes this common law "practical" process when a king was involved in government, with the authority of judges in a democracy—judges simply do not have the same authority to make common law when legislators have created a statute.[317]

In an age in which the U.S. Constitution falls prey to an enticing illusion which by lazy habit finds liberal-minded jurists and the general public applying modern language and context to older language and context, perhaps even for populist purposes, Scalia represents a stern and thin-lipped approach to jurisprudence in general. Unfortunately the only way Scalia's originalism by and large looks both forward and backward is by indicating how today's jurists misinterpret the older law. At center is the assumption that the older lawmakers not only did not conceive of the present context in which their laws now still exist in, but often could not even possibly have imagined it.

One of the most cited examples of Scalia's practice of the originalism philosophy is how he interpreted the Eighth Amendment, specifically, the "cruel and unusual punishment" language, in *Harmelin v. Michigan*.[318] There, Scalia wrote an opinion denying the appeal of a man who had been sentenced to life in prison without the possibility of parole for possession of a little over 650 grams of cocaine. Because the Constitution requires that an improper punishment be both "cruel" and "unusual,"[319] and life in prison is a common (i.e., not "unusual") form of punishment, the issue in *Harmelin* became whether the Eighth Amendment included a "proportionality" element to it (no need to analyze "cruel" here, because if "unusual" flunks, the whole test flunks). Scalia argued it did not and even overruled an earlier three-part proportionality test established only eight years earlier in *Solem v. Helm*.[320]

Scalia's opinion relies on a 1969 article by a Harvard graduate named Anthony Granucci.[321] Although Granucci admits that the drafting of the early bills of rights in the early American colonies, including Virginia's Declaration of Rights which the U.S. Constitution relied on, was "imitative, deficient, and irrationally selective,"[322] he goes on to painstakingly demonstrate that the actual source of the articulation "cruel and unusual" in the Eighth Amendment was a minority statement of the House of Lords to a petition submitted to them by a Protestant cleric named Titus Oates.[323] Only a few years later, this articulation was included verbatim in the English Bill of Rights of 1689.

Granted, tracking the source of what would ultimately become mere "boilerplate"[324] language for the drafting of bills of rights in the early American colonies would entail unavoidably juggling a lot of minor historical events from England. With very little evidence of what lawyers knew when language was copied from an old official document into a new bill of rights, Granucci and Scalia still focus on what the words might generally mean in the context of Oates's situation. Probably 18th-century lawyers did not have before them a neat and tidy comprehensive overview of all usages of the legal ideas of "cruel punishments," let alone "unusual punishments." Nonetheless, by the time the articulation "cruel and unusual" had been added to the U.S. Constitution as inspired by the Virginians, it was 100 years old.

Because Scalia is convinced that "[m]ost historians agree that"[325] the "cruel and unusual" articulation stemmed from the "English Declaration [sic] of Rights,"[326] it must specifically refer to the Oates matter. He even implies that although lawyers who copied the language from one document to the next when drafting their bills of rights or other possible now lost documents had probably never heard of Oates, there is a sort of kernel of legality passed on via *stare decisis* which properly steers the true meaning of the phrase as employed today in a modern Detroit cocaine bust.

Oates's tale harkens back to special penalties invented by George Jeffreys, 1st Baron of Jeffreys (1645-1689), of the King's Bench during the reign of the Catholic King James II. Baron Jeffreys's unpopular misdeeds were aimed at making right Oates's misdeeds in creating a hoax of a conspiracy by Catholics to kill the then Protestant King.[327] Oates had thus been found guilty by Jeffreys of a crime of mere perjury, even though it had led to the deaths of 15 Catholics.[328] By law, Jeffreys could not sentence Oates to death for perjury, but invented a series of punishments that would in essence, so claim certain historians that Scalia cited,[329] serve as a substitute for death. In many ways, Jeffreys was engaging in the same type of roundabout interpretation that the wives of Weinsberg engaged in against King Conrad.[330] In fact, Jeffreys was engaging in what the conservative parable of "going outside the dots" is supposed to prohibit, not to mention originalism itself: bending the law as written to fit what a judge in the context of the moment deems appropriate.

Furthermore, Scalia even specifies that any "vicious punishments" during these "Bloody Assizes"[331] were authorized by common law, such as "drawing and quartering, burning of women felons, beheading, disemboweling, etc."[332] In other words, as long as methods of torture are part of common law, they are certainly not unusual, no matter how cruel, and because the Eighth Amendment includes the word "and," the method must be unusual before it can be in any way unconstitutional.

While Scalia spent much time in *Harmelin* trying to determine that the words "cruel and unusual," even as a textual matter, would only include unusual types of punishment (i.e., against common law), the most important aspect of the case is that this in no way referred to an unusual proportionality of a punishment (i.e., life in prison for possession of 650 grams of cocaine, even when a first offense).[333] Whatever Scalia wanted the word "proportionality" to mean in this context, the ultimate gist of Jeffreys's decree appears to be that among the many punishments heaped upon Oates, only one of them, i.e., defrocking him, should have been deemed unusual, because it was the only punishment that should have been employed by the church, and, therefore, the state had no right to interfere. In addition to this, it was an unusual punishment that had never been a punishment for perjury.

In the end, the argument about proportionality turns out to probably be the most important issue in *Harmelin*, as compared with Oates. Based on the severity of the punishment of the death penalty for perjury during the 1600s (as opposed to the punishment eventually meted out to

Oates—life in prison, among other public humiliations), Jeffreys was not allowed to initially give Oates the death penalty—based generally on the same philosophy of proportionality and due process that Scalia addresses later in his *Harmelin* opinion. The unusualness of using the death penalty for a charge of perjury in the 1600s is a matter of proportionality, because, based on Scalia's own argument, there was nothing unusual about the death penalty in common law. Meanwhile, Oates's case in no way involved some of the more Medieval methods of torture left to the imagination here, other than whipping and a regular appearance in the pillory.[334]

Even if "most historians" (as per Scalia's uncited presumption[335]) consider the words "cruel and unusual" to mean something that excludes a proportionality test based on what the words were originally intended to portray, as well as its subsequent historical usage, Scalia acknowledges his opponents in recognizing what seems to be a big exception to this exclusion in death penalty cases. In fact, Scalia still affirms at the end of his opinion in *Harmelin* that "required mitigation" (clearly using what otherwise seems to be proportionality as to severity of a crime before it deserves the death penalty) is properly part of the death penalty jurisprudence as per "cruel and unusual," especially the appeals process of death penalty cases based on the Eighth Amendment as to proportionality. Nonetheless, for Scalia, this is still not necessarily based on an exception, but on the "unique"[336] nature of the death penalty, along with the two varieties of life-in-prison sentences: with or without the possibility of parole. Scalia anticipates the argument from opponents that mitigating whether to apply the death penalty or not belongs to a scale that measures severity. Any such measure of severity therefore involves a proportionality factor whenever a death penalty is appealed based on the Eighth Amendment.[337]

Not only this, Scalia goes on to rate the severity of the three most severe punishments: the death penalty being the most severe; life in prison without the possibility of parole is the second most severe; and life in prison with the possibility of parole is third most severe.[338] Even though this could be the start of a top-ten "most severe punishment" list and therefore a proportionality test, Scalia wriggles out of the trap by claiming that these are three distinct punishments that happen to be able to be rated together in severity. In using the word "unique" artfully and according to its correct definition, that is, meaning "something that there is only one of," Scalia first disqualifies all three of these punishments as being anything that a scale could be used to measure. If it is unique, there is only one of it, and therefore it cannot be compared to anything else—therefore no proportionality.

On the other hand, if the two types of life in prison are not proportional, Harmelin would have a case that the Eighth Amendment should apply. Therefore, in the final sentence of the opinion, Scalia backtracks and then "draws the line"[339] at the death penalty, after reminding us that "flexible techniques" in the sentencing reduction process (such as executive clemency or legislative changes) make even life sentences proportional to any other sentence.

In this way, by claiming the uniqueness of the death penalty is proportionality as the only proportionality test under "cruel and unusual," *Harmelin* remains safely outside the jurisdiction of the Eighth Amendment, because life in prison without parole would involve a proportionality test other than the unique death penalty proportionality.[340] With a touch of religious irony, this conclusion also skirts precariously around the original proportionality ethic of the Judeo-Christian culture of *lex talionis*, or an "eye for an eye,"[341] despite Scalia's strong Catholicism.

Nonetheless, it appears that much of the power in the words of originalism derive not from the meaning of the words themselves, but simply from the fact that extensive research into the history of certain lingual phrases provides us with an unexpected explanation of their source. Originalists like Scalia go on to argue that a judge must honor such historical sources as a remote, almost subliminal form of *stare decisis*. That "cruel and unusual" is also used in Justice Thurgood Marshall's dissent in *Harmelin* as grounds to find the death penalty unconstitutional altogether, demonstrates that Scalia's elaborate explanation about original meaning has by no means silenced any opponents. Also noteworthy is the lack of similar harsh originalism in Scalia's defense of the right to own guns in his Second Amendment interpretation in *District of Columbia v. Heller*.[342]

In fact, it is nothing less than an amateurish mistake in the study of anything that involves past usages and events, whether it is philology, genealogy, musicology, philosophy, or especially law, to assume that however words and phrases are employed over the centuries, the changes that inevitably occur in their meaning are somehow related to a laziness that must to the best of the ability of living scholars be corrected. Ricœur had a similar battle against logical positivists to exonerate usage of the metaphor in language.[343] As an example, allow the title of a famous novel by Robert Louis Stevenson to demonstrate that our legal world does not suffer, is not inefficient, is not inarticulate, is not unscholarly, and most definitely is not lazy if it continues to refer to the crime of kidnapping as any asportation by force of another, typically for a ransom (originally, the crime referred to forcing someone onto a ship in an effort to take them out of the country for the purpose of involuntary servitude).[344]

Above all, etymologies are provided in dictionaries not necessarily to only enrich our understanding of a word, but to allow us to be aware of past usages. The fact that so many modern words have a checkered past in terms of slang usage by no means makes use of the word today any less legitimate.

Moreover, the originalism argument might raise the same sort of question that the issue of fides informis raises in theology: is there a faith in the law here without an essential living element, that in theology is referred to as a "faith without love."[345] Ultimately, this argument does have merit against originalism, even from a more secular point of view.

Whatever charm Neo-Conservatives have in demonstrating a love and respect for the past among friends of like mind often strikes other observers as indulgent and shallow paternalism. Rescuing certain facts from obscurity and putting them on display inside of a legal opinion of the Supreme Court may create its own sort of historical curiosity for all time, but as binding law preserved by *stare decisis*, these curiosities also share something with the experience of a carnival where relics and oddities of the past continue their relevance to modern times by being displayed in jars of formaldehyde.

SKEPTICISM AS A BRANCH OF HERMENEUTICS

Without outright questioning the originalists' motives—motives that as a roundabout way might be a way of achieving the Neo-Conservative goal of limiting the role of the Federal government—a hermeneut eventually might reluctantly agree that if Scalia is appealing to his own sense of phronesis and is in good faith seeing the world the way that is reflected in his opinions, there is little to criticize further about his logic from a hermeneutical point of view. He is in fact his own version of a hermeneut, and, as a duly appointed judge, his iconoclastic interpretation of the law stands, even if he is paradoxically criticizing judges for legislating from the bench at the same time.

Although a personal acknowledgement of phronesis is by no means license to project whatever meaning to a law might be convenient to achieve something from an entirely different agenda, the fallacy of questioning someone's motives bases itself on the assumption that the critic is trying to prove that the other person's argument is "wrong." If Scalia believes his own arguments, as shortsighted as they may be, questioning the motives of a Neo-Conservative judge nevertheless does not prove his arguments are "wrong."

Nonetheless, Gadamer's indirect voice as a critic of the burgeoning world of originalism during the 1970s did not come without a proviso provided from another prominent voice from Continental Europe. In 1967, Habermas had expressed his own argument against Gadamer in terms of his way of using hermeneutics resting on the prejudices that are formed by culture and tradition, including what is commonly considered authority.

At one crucial point in his argument, Habermas adamantly opposed any convergence between "authority" and "understanding" (Authorität und Erkenntnis konvergieren nicht).[346] Some onlookers looking to simplify the situation have even allowed a very rough interpretation of this row as Habermas criticizing Gadamer as a student of Heidegger, when embedded deep inside the latter's philosophy must have been some sort of distorted sympathy for Nazi ideology.[347] Although this gross simplification might even portray Habermas as somehow representing the liberal, or even Marxist, point of view, complete with the association that he is from Frankfurt am Main, and the Frankfurt School (Horkheimer, Adorno, and others),[348] the dispute still stands today as a form of pure philosophical impasse, sanitized from any "real existing" pernicious events from history such as Nazis or Communists.

Introducing Ricœur's notion "hermeneutics of suspicion" (les **herméneutiques du soupçon**[349]) at this point may not lend clarity to the relationship between hermeneutics and originalism, but Ricœur did intend to show that behind the Habermas-Gadamer contretemps was the same inquisitive scholarship that led Marx, Nietzsche, and Freud into their directions of questioning (or being suspicious of) a status quo. Meanwhile, Scalia's point of view is just as suspicious of the status quo as these three were (if not more).

Using Marx, Nietzsche, and Freud as muses in this pursuit has drawbacks, because these figures still unfortunately incite controversy. Meanwhile, Ricœur's triumvirate of "suspicious" thinkers had their own subliminal forces to their philosophies, suggesting they were driven more by a mixture of suspicion and faith, than turning away from tradition: for Marx, it was the obvious but unacknowledged influence of Christian charity in sharing; for Nietzsche, it was the genuine and ongoing conflict which he only partially acknowledged in weaning himself from what he saw as a vulgarization of Germanic tradition by his childhood idol, composer Richard Wagner[350]; and for Freud, it was the unacknowledged influence of the writings of the Marquis de Sade, whose 1788 short story "Florville et Courval, ou le Fatalisme"[351] portrays the Oedipus complex long before any fin-de-siècle Viennese influences had taken shape.

In fact, the concept of a "School of Suspicion" (Schule des Verdachts) can be found in Nietzsche's writings.[352] Skeptical inquiry itself has been the impetus behind ideas as diverse as Descartes's *cogito* to Einstein's energy-mass conversion.

As merely affirming a deliberate methodology to attain a hidden intention behind what might otherwise appear to be spontaneous, Ricœur's observations did not take sides between Gadamer and Habermas. He saw the difference between the two modern German minds with roots in a horrible German past as an opportunity to settle something larger.

Nonetheless, Ricœur employs the concept of "distanciation"[353] into this dialogue, referring here to the alienation of an individual to tradition. This was the state of mind, he says, in which Marx, Nietzsche, and Freud, not to mention to some degree Habermas, prepared their philosophies in order to break free from a "false consciousness"[354] of their day.

Even though Heidegger had his own ideas about this concept (Verfremdung or Seinsvergessenheit[355]), his student Gadamer's philosophy revolves around the importance of a sense of "belonging" (Zughörigkeit[356]) to tradition, according to Ricœur. Although these stances ostensibly are supposed to conflict with one another, both Gadamer and Ricœur reveal that their methods involve several different steps of giving and taking, so that there really should not be any discord between these notions of alienation and belonging.

Interestingly enough, Gadamer also spoke about a concept of "belonging" in connection with Aristotle's notion of the theater, and how the listener tunes into the drama by losing a sense of reality.[357] It was Bertolt Brecht (1898-1956) who made famous his concept of theater diametrically opposed to Aristotle's in the "alienation effect" (Verfremdungseffekt or V-effekt), hoping his theater-goers would be completely disoriented and not be able to identify with the character on stage.[358] Marx also used a similar term (Entfremdung[359]) to describe the general isolation of the worker to the products of his work.

It is also important to point out that in German, the word "Fremd" emphasizes something especially foreign or removed from culture or tradition. Suffice it to say, there is certainly a wide chasm between how Gadamer distinguishes the quality of being "foreign," when the text involved actually needs to be translated,[360] and the quality in theater that Brecht was striving for, symbolic of many things: from alienation of the classes in the political world; to the beauty achieved in Japanese theater by alienating the actors from the audience.[361]

Habermas uses the concept of "alienation" (Verfremdung[362]) to distinguish reflective understanding from the everyday understanding subscribed by positivism that leads to false objectification of an experience in reality. In this, Habermas and Gadamer appear to agree, as Habermas goes on to explain that the "truth" (Wahrheit) and "method" (Methode) in the title of Gadamer's book represent the joining of the philosophical and scientific.[363] That Ricœur steps into this by forming his own sense in "distanciation," that appears to borrow more from Marx than any of the other references, as something as opposed to tradition and therefore shut off from the culture that custom and tradition are the results of, affirms alienation without embracing it.

The result of this is the "false consciousness," which in the case of Freud especially, implies that some other secret agenda is lurking subliminally. That embracing tradition can lead to a sense of belonging that can indeed be false actually does sum up what Habermas might have been criticizing Gadamer for.

Ricœur's hermeneutics succeed in providing a more complete picture for the next generation of hermeneuts, who actually found renewed interest in Marx, Nietzsche, and Freud and their applications as steps in the hermeneutical process. In a word of caution, it also strangely encourages conspiracy theorists, who by habit always question what they are told in the form of an "official version."

In all these ways, Scalia also works to combat his own sense of false consciousness by distancing himself from the status quo—what he sees as a lazy and undeveloped sense of statutory and constitutional interpretation. Like Brecht, his opinions often deliberately alienate the reader by appealing to obscure historical events, when all along such illustrations serve mostly to allow the judge to disqualify himself as not having the authority from a Democratic government to legislate from the bench—and, also like Brecht, filled with plenty of drama and theatrical effect. Despite what Scalia assures us is the popular mandate, most voters in this Democracy during the 1980s were probably unaware that access to the courts with genuine injustices might cease, based on a Justice's unemotional ruling that there is no longer a power to the court that existed when common law was first formed in England centuries ago.

Indeed, Neo-Conservatives proved themselves as the same sort of iconoclasts as Marx, Nietzsche, and Freud, but the hermeneut still wonders about the foundation that Scalia's views rest on—namely that a text can ever be dead, beyond interpretation. Ultimately, textualism and orginalism must make the distinction between alienation and simply being on display as a dead object. Information in any form, let alone a text, always requires the living and breathing to process its meaning, or, like the Zen Koan about the tree falling in the woods when no one hears it, there is no meaning without the process of phronesis and interpretation.

CHAPTER THREE

A Postmodern Approach

WHAT IS MODERNISM?

Aside from its general definition to mean anything occurring presently, the word "modernism" as describing some sort of trend in thinking and activity usually starkly compares and contrasts something old (unmodern) with something new (modern). Because the old usually is familiar, the new is introduced as something strange and even at times counterintuitive. Different versions of modernism also compete with each other, since historically only one true path of thinking into the future will prevail.

By now, most people recognize certain crucial moments in history that radically changed the old way of looking at things, what was until then a normal way of looking at things. For example, when it was discovered that the world was round and not flat, this formerly counterintuitive notion radically altered everyone's perception of reality. At that point, there was an urgency that everyone accept the new modern way of looking at things. In other words, in order to be a modern human being, it was necessary to adopt this new way of thinking.

In the 20th-century especially, this urgency drove many different new ideas, such as evolution, Einstein's Theory of Relativity, Freud, Marxism, as well as in some circles new approaches to faith, which average people did not fully understand but could be convinced were new ways of thinking superior to the old ways—new ways of thinking that had to be accepted in order to be modern or "up to date." This faith in the new often allowed critics to claim that modernism suffered from a sort of "Emperor's new clothes" syndrome: everyone claimed to understand the importance of the new ideas without really understanding them at all.

More importantly, there was a sense to modernism that "well enough could not be left alone" or that perfectly functional and competent ideas were being tinkered with in the spirit of making them more "modern." This was especially true in the field of art, because the old art was being preserved and enjoyed in a substantial new way via modern printing, audio recording, and eventually computers. At times, the tendency to experiment made certain perfectly functional ideas more complicated and esoteric than it appeared to the layperson they needed to be. In fact, postmodernism itself often became driven by the same urgency and forces as a new way of thinking that people now had to adopt. This was one of many contradictions that postmodernism always inherently and stubbornly preserved, no matter how ardently the thinker acting as theorist claimed to understand this new way of thinking.

Whether an era called "modernism" began in the Renaissance,[364] the Age of Enlightenment, the early 20th-century, or whether it even existed as an "era" at all but more as an ongoing way of thinking does not matter. New modern ideas that radically advance civilization go back to the discovery of fire. What does matter is the universal notion of supporting the advancement of civilization by finding ever more new ideas that will improve and even replace the old ideas. In fact, the instinct to conquer one's foe, especially if that foe is an old and oppressive empire, is one of the oldest universal notions in history—a longing for one's ethnicity or country to be so great that it will conquer the world.

WHAT IS POSTMODERNISM?

Various disciplines have adopted the term "postmodernism" to mean slightly different things, but usually it clearly can relate to some sort of regress, symbolic or otherwise, in the urgency to develop and advance new ideas. In architecture during the 1940s, it referred to using human contours in a building rather than the prevailing square, machine metaphors of buildings of the early 20th-century like the Empire State Building.[365] During the 1960s, music adopted the term to refer to the end of a necessity to find new styles, allowing musical collages consisting of old styles, pastiche, and a general blurring between high-brow and low-brow cultures.[366] In philosophy, the old rigid process of legitimation of scientific maxims has been softened in light of the game of language that cannot be avoided to describe it, but also the prospect that computers will provide scientific discoveries and store them as information.[367]

Although postmodernism is different in this clearly non-exhaustive list of the three above examples, there is a common thread: in architecture, using the machine metaphor in designing buildings represents a techno-logically pure system with all of the certainty and rigidity that properly functioning machinery provides; in music, there is no ultimate prevail-ing style (system of music) representing the most advanced style, corre-sponding to the mechanical accuracy and certainty in architecture; and in philosophy, understanding the ultimate scientific system can only be through the imperfections of language, which require tolerance for many explanations of smaller phenomena without even attempting a single, universal explanation for how it all fits in the macrocosm. The regress in all three examples away from finding a new and improved system (if not once and for all a perfect system) leads to almost a surrender to continue the older imperfect systems even if in a contradictory, counterintuitive way.

Although there are as many possible starting points as to when post-modernism began, the year 1975 is probably more convenient than most, corresponding roughly with the end of the Vietnam War. At this point in time, the Liberal voice in America shifted radically, because it had to adapt a new way of thinking without the convenience of the continuing injustice of this unpopular war. The already named but amorphously de-fined entity called postmodern philosophy served as some sort of heir apparent to fill the void. In light of the more narrow (modern) affirmation of capitalism in the looming Libertarian and Neo-Conservative currents of that time, it certainly did not have to be out of step with the diversity of postmodernism, as long as the postmodernist is considering all the points of view available in his or her landscape, even if they happen to fall into older ones following the more modern ideal.

The allure of postmodernism is at the same time the very problem with it: it focuses on the unavoidable contradictions inherent in reality as rep-resented by language by contradicting itself. No one in their right mind could ever actually believe that when the Berlin Wall fell in 1989 that Francis Fukuyama's postmodern statement that it represented the "end of history"[368] somehow meant that time itself stopped ticking. So does postmodernism even exist?

WHAT IS POSTMODERNISM IN LAW?

The most notable outcome of postmodernism as applied to law is a change in the way the Rule of Law has required a consistent and universal application and enforcement.[369] For example, the racial contra-dictions and ramifications of the Indian Child Welfare Act demonstrate how racism is generally held to be unconstitutional on the one hand, but allowed when it is necessary for the preservation of a culture.[370] In other words, contradictory policies lead to black-letter laws that also appear to contradict each other, but must be upheld nonetheless for justice to prevail, despite the feeling of one class of people seeming to be given a privilege that another class does not get.

Those who have attempted an adaptation of postmodern thinking to law tend to emphasize the exploration of philosophy as a language game,[371] which is convenient as applied to law since language remains a crucial part of all legal thinking and practice. In essence, three general categories have been helpful in narrowing down the discussion of this game as applied to postmodern law, so that it might lead to a consensus even though contradictions are still ubiquitous: 1) narrative, 2) legitimation, and 3) differend.

This chapter will further develop these three words before attempting to assess whether postmodernism is an era that, however well it has served to further more intellectual thinking in law, is now coming to an end. If the end of postmodernism is indeed near, perhaps a glimpse into the future as to what will replace or attenuate it will be possible.

NARRATIVE

The most confusing aspect about postmodernism then remains how the entire trend is not only a work in progress, while thinkers scramble through the philosophies of the 20th-century continuously looking for new ideas to add to the ongoing dialogue, but also an era no one really has any idea how to end, because no one really knows for certain what it is. The basic idea of tolerance for different opinions without a metanarrative that all opinions should yield to has endless variations as to what social theory, art, or even law should look like, but eventually there must be an end to this freedom and a return to the discernment that not everyone can be right. In fact, it is probably through the law that the postmodern bubble will most likely pop first (if it hasn't already), based almost entirely on a renewed sense that injustice should not occur. And why should efforts to avoid injustice not be a universal pursuit?

Up to now, this article reflects great pains taken to begin with a simplified definition of modernism and postmodernism. In that spirit, narrative serves as the basic and most simple building block of both.

As a concept purely in the abstract, narrative provides a general idea that allows a distinct continuity in the representations of ideas formulated by experiences in reality that have been accumulated as knowledge. Just as walking a straight line requires a human being to put one foot in front of the other within an interval of time, a narrative similarly allows events to bind themselves together in time, and through a mysterious process of concatenation, appear as a single idea or unity. Narratives then become playing pieces in a language game that can be moved around the board to formulate either a philosophy favoring modernism or one favoring postmodernism.

At the end of the 1970s, when Lyotard contributed his own take on postmodernism in a book called *La Condition postmoderne*,[372] which appeared in 1984 in English as *The Postmodern Condition*,[373] his interpretation had the effect of all but exclusively annexing the entire topic and dialogue of postmodernism up to that point, especially in terms of how postmodernism applied to law.[374] He proposed Marxism as one of two basic examples of representational models for society in the mid-20th-century, the one most demonstrating how society naturally divides into two parts: class struggle and dialectics.[375] (Talcott Parsons was cited as the other example, in which society functions as a whole without division.[376]) In light of Lyotard's now quintessential work, Marxism stood as an ongoing example of a "great master narrative" legitimizing political militants for a new social order, but mostly because Marxism espouses that there is some radically different alternative to capitalism in the future.[377] Because overcoming the depredations of real existing capitalism, even in its most rudimentary or popularized form, at least appeared to be an all-encompassing and inescapable universal norm, Lyotard proposed and implemented the term "metanarrative" as an important part of the methodology required to legitimize knowledge itself through a philosophy of history.[378] Marxism was also a metanarrative, because it proposed how history should enfold in the future to reinforce the ongoing progress of civilization, but it was a grand narrative, in that it was a total science that like Newtonian physics aimed at describing a specific category of reality in a universal way.

At first, grand narratives became Lyotard's postmodernist's bogeyman because it did not allow the tolerance for trial-and-error detours along the way once the laws were in place.[379] Instead, the primacy of the narrative itself, or story-telling in the microcosm, became the focus of Lyotard's philosophy.[380] Above all, it was the vast diversity of narratives and how even contradicting narratives could exist together as useful sources of describing one event.

This trend in thinking probably prevailed in Lyotard's writings because of the curious enticement of a contradictory nature of the youngest notion of early postmodernism: by trying to overcome predominant ideas that were once considered modern, postmodernism functions as if it were its own modern and predominant idea. The temporal aspect of the word "modernism" as something happening "now" makes for confusion and contradiction once postmodernists imply that what they are doing is what is happening "now." For Lyotard, the old notion that Marx represented a projected future that legitimated its knowledge for everyone, because they were all struggling to attain such a future, is what prevailed under modernism. Somehow, postmodernism allowed for much more: trial and error once a law was in place, but with seemingly nothing but errors made and nonetheless retained and reused along the way when making projections about what a future would or even should be.

Of course, Lyotard was not the first to apply postmodernism to the law, but somehow the word meant many different things to so many thinkers such as Ihab Hassan (defining postmodernism as a sort of "typology of void" in literature[381]), Michel Foucault (rounding out his historical eras, with modernism beginning in the Renaissance and concepts of "archeology" and Nietzschean "genealogy" used in nonconventional ways to describe new approaches to analysis[382]), Gilles Deleuze and Félix Guattari (forming together a system that appears to glorify but control concepts analyzing schizophrenia, desire, and an elusive unit of chaos dubbed the "rhizome"[383]), Jean Baudrillard (sharing Fukuyama's vision of a vanishing history[384]), and Fredric Jameson (attempting to distinguish extreme postmodernism from "reconstructive" postmodernism[385]). Even Lyotard eventually yielded to the approach by Ernesto Laclau and Chantal Mouffe that postmodernism had not replaced modernism, but included it and all other older ways of thinking under the postmodern umbrella.[386] Unlike Humpty Dumpty, when the theories of these postmodernists seem to break into a million pieces, as well as any alliances they might have among each other, those pieces always tend to mend themselves back together again to form the ongoing, ever-changing postmodern narrative.

Nothing about this formative process soundly brought about a consistency or consensus as to what postmodernism is, but even any disagreement about it among those who intelligently espoused it was embraced as a sort of byproduct of the elusive word. Each version was in essence its own narrative, and according to postmodernism, each narrative had to be honored. The impact of such a remarkable free-for-all was in itself its own type of syncretic narrative, even if consensus, which became an important topic among these postmodernists, was nowhere to be found.

Somehow it all reflected the indecipherable nature of the world itself at the brink of some sort of metamorphosis helped along by the unpredictable momentum of an ongoing advancement in technological applications in computers, while struggling against a sort of anti-momentum regarding the mysteries of an ongoing impasse in basic scientific research into subatomic particles versus new scientific impasses regarding mapping of the stars and dark matter. Even early on, by the 1990s, certain critics who had mastered the famous books that had formed this postmodern path began to further pick it apart with further painstaking and voluble prose, but not before putting all it back together again.[387]

In the thrill and excitement of it all, somehow caution over throwing babies out with bathwater had little effect as philosophers and their philosophies were rearranged and reordered like so many pieces of nonmatching furniture in a large room. Under modernism, Freud had a central place as a prophet of liberated desire, while Nietzsche came off as a jack-of-all-trades in the project of decentralizing ideas, as his aphorisms tend to still stand as an example of how consciousness had been fragmented into disparate parts.

Even more importantly, Marx suddenly appeared to be the symbol of everything old, while economics and capitalism were redefined as vanguards of some revived new reality. Fascism still lurked here and there, even behind images of commercialism, but the burning concern of not repeating what the Nazis had done during World War II became almost an old-fashioned guilt that could be overcome with a few minor tweaks of one's conscience without venturing into the hell of immorality. Although the neo-modern equations of the Chicago School of Economics profoundly challenged the more circuitous chains of logic that postmodernism appeared to espouse, the postmodernists still played a stubborn hand of tolerance, not sparring with the new Libertarians and their army of Ayn Rand[388] survivalists.

Whether opposing it or embracing it, postmodernism allowed an observer to say just about anything about it that might form some sort of almost musical or poetic coherence, because pinning down consensus as to what it all means was all but irrelevant. Lyotard's bringing in Kant as a foundation further added to the notion that the same Western philosophy, especially German idealism, that had been taken so seriously for so many years despite an ongoing difficulty of understanding what it actually meant was suddenly becoming something full of free associations of meaning. The gaudiness surrounding postmodern pastiche even began flavoring this once solemn tradition of Western philosophy including all of its dour faces on marble busts with the colors and textures of comic book characters.

On the other hand, denying the academic politics of it all fell into yet another exercise in liberating the mind to postmodernism, but more likely, ignored how the juxtaposition of these thinkers was taking the form of a secret handshake. Postmodernists, like any other academic discipline of the last half of the 20th-century, required anyone who wanted to be a part of the movement to name off the important thinkers (such as "Lyotard," "Deleuze," "Baudrillard," et al.) as a prelude to any worthwhile discourse that might add or subtract from what was fast becoming a sacred canon of postmodernism. The question remains whether this academic part of postmodernism was just another defect, or if it actually had become a part of the postmodern narrative itself. Like any other secret handshake, a newbie would never receive back the glint in the eye of the established postmodern beholder, but oddly enough, the newbie should always be a part of the postmodern narrative even if he never has any intention of learning the secret handshake. In this way, the more famous among the postmodernism movement morphed it into a free form of esoteric heuristic that kept only its participants among the powerful few, while continuously espousing that any newbie's narrative was just as important. That made postmodernism a sort of model of a politic so transparent it was practically invisible and an average onlooker could barely see into it, only if to ultimately learn, upon further deliberation, that he was actually inside of it looking out.

Striking what appeared to be a final death knell of Marxism with the fall of the Berlin Wall in 1989 and the collapse of the Soviet Union in 1990, with some of the more established postmodernists scrambling for dry ground, newer voices such as Fukuyama's[389] ominously found new ground for postmodernism at least slightly redefined. Such overwhelming and powerful narratives as Fukuyama's when helped along by the American press further added to what was becoming the collective comic book imagery of mass media narratives delivered by colorful talking head commentators.

On the other hand, that has not silenced other postmodernists like Gianni Vattimo from formulating new narratives, especially in terms of newly elected Marxist leaders in Latin America as the 21st-century dawned.[390] One narrative that included Venezuelan President Hugo Chávez calling the President of the United States George W. Bush a "devil," suggested possible retaliations, even veiled threats of U.S.-instigated assassination attempts.[391] The same American President asserted an alliance with a reluctant President and General Pervez Musharraf of Pakistan, even though the latter had once blamed the American CIA for the terrorist attacks on September 11, 2001, and supported the very enemy the alliance's purpose was to destroy: the Taliban (the same former President Musharraf faced the death penalty after a trial for treason which was only overturned in the year 2020).[392] As reported in modern media, each postmodern narrative paints each situation with broad strokes of good guys and bad guys, but fails to reckon the entire world's events into a universal whole so that sentiments themselves indeed do not contradict each other.

If postmodernism is indeed tolerant of such contradictory sentiments in the process of embracing all narratives, even if contradictory, as viable microcosms that when considered altogether produce the closest thing to a universal whole, hasn't it been simply a reinvention of nihilism, at least at the microcosmic level, or "Anything Goes"? At some point, the macrocosms step in to curb its tolerance and declare certain things untruths, but then we are back to square one and talking in terms of universalism, metanarratives, and grand narratives.

Still, the language game poses these much more difficult questions in terms of narrative, while something else that uses narrative, like music, makes its claims to narrative without ever having to contradict itself.[393] Instead of contradictions, one version of postmodern music dealt with clashing preexisting musical styles against each other into a collage—one style did not "belong" with the other. If this trend in music is any indication, it would suggest that any truths or even aesthetic judgment to be ascertained through the lens of the postmodern thinker has to do with treating the separate narratives as secondary in meaning, if not already dead in terms of their original meanings, in and of themselves, but which live when combined with other narratives into a newly formed whole.

These types of questions concerning the very nature of narrative require yet more borrowing from disciplines such as sociology, anthropology, religion, history and even the law and literature movement. Sociologist Hayden White (1928-2018) narrowed the nature of narrative down to "knowing" somehow converted into a "telling,"[394] specifying that unlike other types of writing, narrative is easy to translate from one language to the next.[395] In this way, narrative is a simple form of discourse and tends to limited itself to only the third person singular and a couple of tenses, such as the preterit or pluperfect.[396] The further purity of events that "really happened" (i.e., not imaginary or myth) which are told by a distinct "teller" who is most often never referred to in the narrative itself, forms one of the crucial building blocks of at least historiography in its most basic form, if not other forms of common discourse. That is, of course, not to say that history must always be told in a narrative form; historians are free to use other types of discourse. Still, historians thrive for an accuracy, and vouch for it, which implies that certain narratives can be inaccurate or false. Historians can make things up out of mischief, or can make genuine mistakes. They can also simply not know about certain stretches of the past and make things up out of utility. If postmodernists are so sensitive about history, how can there possibly be a trend of tolerance for differing narratives?

Lyotard himself has framed this question precisely and accurately as the one Achilles heel of postmodernism that will not go away, especially in the form of injustice:

> "It is not true that one can do an aesthetic politics. It is not true the search for intensities or things of that type can ground politics, because there is the problem of injustice. It is not true, for example, that once one has gotten rid of the primacy of the understanding in its knowing function, there is only aesthetic judgment left to discriminate between the just and the unjust. Aesthetic judgment allows the discrimination of that which pleases from that which does not please. With justice, we have to do, of necessity, with the regulation of something else."[397]

Although a reaffirmation of desire and will as genuine human experience might allow an unleashing of curiosity and passions that do not include the arbitrary patience of building a single unidirectional society, a human will and desire to do an injustice still cannot stand.

On the other hand, just as Lyotard had zeroed in on the problem of postmodernism, the problem resurrects itself in precisely the very conflicts that originally gave birth to postmodernism. Lyotard's complex philosophical treatise of Neo-Kantian and Hellenistic thought called *the Differend*[398] invites the reader to mull over the genuine problem that one act in the name of justice can create several injustices. Two parties in dispute might reach a solution that does not wipe away injustice, but mitigates it for one party to a more tolerable level, while putting the other party at an even lower but impliedly tolerable level of injustice. Our justice system depends upon the mass media narrative that the justice system, like an auto mechanic, takes in matters of dispute and fixes them into well-running, high performance vehicles. When the jury speaks, justice is done, and the situation is "fixed." Lyotard's journey through the problems of the differend and injustice hit the postmodern nail so firmly on the head, that it will require further analysis in the third part of this chapter.

Just the same, if multifarious and even contradictory narratives function as building blocks in the microcosmic level of a reality that will never march in one direction, has the law really recognized this and if so, how will the Wizard-of-Oz illusion that modern society maintains justice through its legal system (the main concept behind "legitimation") stand the shock that justice is an elusive and unattainable metanarrative?

Postmodernism demonstrates this problem, so if there is no solution in sight, is postmodernism the final resting point of all philosophical inquiry? Calling this dilemma an aporia, as postmodernists do, ties it down in a seemingly temporary way, but also feigns a control over something that is still intellectually, scientifically, and even socially without control or understanding. In fact, there is really no difference in this confrontation with aporia than Wittgenstein's famous final sentence in his *Logische-Philosphische Abhandlung*.[399]

One insightful maverick who gave the concept "narrative" a central position in his by and large postmodern thinking of law and philosophy was Robert Cover (1943-1986), although he never otherwise embraced the rubric postmodernism or endorsed its adherents by name. In his essay "Nomos and Narrative,"[400] Cover cryptically but with clear deliberateness demonstrates how precepts of law which are in essence all but written in stone can invent its own exceptions through the power of sacred narratives, such as those in the Bible. Stories of the respected forbears of people in a community bound by a sense of history, if not race, that are preserved through the power of myth and tradition depict these honored forbears as using guile and "human deceit"[401] to break the law. Referring to the law with the Greek word "nomos," Cover explains that it is the combination of the concrete precepts versus the law-breaking stories that combine to form a "typology of reversal."[402] This is similar to how the postmodernists use narratives to overcome a sense of foundationalism and an ultimate totality.

In this way, what has prevailed under the allusive rubric of postmodernism in law resembles a state of affairs that has long existed as an alternative to the brutality of the sovereign conqueror. The tendency to view any one king as being the same as any other overlooks those exceptions in history where a conqueror did not engage in utter genocide or the destruction of a conquered people's language, religion, and culture. There are ways a king may rule over the conquered people that do not involve putting them in outright slavery with an aim of getting them to speak the sovereign language, practice the sovereign religion, and otherwise accept the sovereign culture. Prodigious examples of this in history include when the Persians allowed the Jews to go back to their temple in Jerusalem and practice their religion after centuries of slavery under the Babylonians and Medes,[403] but also the concept of Federalism in the United States Constitution.[404] On the other hand, if the U.S. Constitution is a product of the Enlightenment and therefore under the postmodern regime a product of modernity, how would a postmodern constitution differ? Under such an analogy, the 50 States of America serve as 50 narratives whose diversity in laws and traditions are allowed to flourish on their own.

So if history has already produced examples of conflicting and contradicting narratives that can coexist in an ultimate entity that does not force them to conform to the point of utter assimilation, except when absolutely necessary, did postmodernism invent anything new, or was it simply some sort of reinvention in light of new technology and/or new oppressive politics in light of the post-Vietnam era? If Lyotard's vision involved tolerating the conflicting and contradicting narratives at the microcosm, did he fail to see that postmodernism itself serves as the grand narrative, even though it remains unfocused and undefined? This still remains a crucial and key argument toward moving beyond this overall trend of postmodernism.

If there is one thing that postmodernism in law preserves over the tolerance of the Enlightenment, it is that language games and all its contradictions as part of the overall structuring of a theory of law prevails, as it does in a postmodern society as a whole. The U.S. Constitution of the Enlightenment makes for a bold statement in history as to tolerating the different narratives of its now 50 States, but introducing mechanisms that allow for even more conflicting and contradicting laws and policies is probably the best way to describe what the postmodern revolution has tried to accomplish. Precisely what such mechanisms would be has yet to be determined.

LEGITIMATION

The process of legitimizing norms into laws once they are determined by consensus is actually something that Kant championed in Western philosophy—one of the crucial factors of the Enlightenment, along with predominance of objective science and independent art. This process of legitimation emphasizing democracy now stands as a foil against postmodernism, especially from the works of Habermas, despite the fact that Lyotard's ideas are ultimately developed through Neo-Kantianism as well.

Aside from an actual process that initiates laws into a society, there is also the aspect of maintaining the legitimacy, once enacted. Through various forms of lethargy, cynicism, and processes that become arbitrary and meaningless, legitimacy can lose its power.[405]

Such problems of legitimation of a state are also what drove postmodernists into criticizing the ideal of the consensus as not always maintaining or even achieving legitimacy, in that a more powerful position can often sway others into a consensus they don't really want. Still, Habermas has distinguished himself from postmodernism by thoroughly critiquing the problems of legitimation, as well as discourse, into two guiding principles: facticity (Faktizität) and validation (Geltung).[406]

Throughout Habermas's critique of such problems of legitimation, the importance of discourse, or discourse theory, includes narrative, but also other forms of discourse, such as the philosophical and the economic. Specifically, his idea of communicative action (Handeln) stands as the most fundamental position in his philosophy.[407] In fact, communicative action is so fundamental in a philosophy of legitimation and law, he emphasizes it is also ahistorical. In other words, Marxism emphasized a certain imminence as to how history forces us to form philosophical solutions, while Habermas insists that such imminence is no longer relevant, because of a breakdown and cynicism of the bourgeoisie that is so critical to legitimating democracy.[408]

The essence of the rift between Habermas's philosophy of communicative action and the postmodernists has to do with whether Habermas's position is simply some sort of a modification of modernism and the Enlightenment, and therefore not anything postmodernist at all. Habermas also has proved in the past (against Gadamer, for example) that he has a quick trigger finger when it comes to associating certain philosophies with fascism, such as Nietzsche and Heidegger.[409] The tendency with Habermas is to associate postmodernism first with a type of conservatism, because it somehow is supposed to go against modernity, but second with irrationality and anarchy.

Although there are certainly things about fascism that make it a mystical or irrational point of view, as well as an anti-democratic point of view, it makes for an overgeneralized confusion when attempting to sort out exactly the position politically that postmodernists have been taking. Although Libertarianism in America could be safely considered a conservative philosophy (despite some who disingenuously insist it is an optimal blending of both liberal and conservative), based on an anti-democratic stance adverse to government in general, their ranks rarely espouse anything that appears to be postmodern or the doctrines of postmodernists, let alone "irrationalists." In fact, the selling point of Libertarianism is that there is a rational way to run a business and the individual can do it better than a government.[410]

These subtle shades of political greys make it easy to misconstrue at least the political stance of an opponent espousing postmodernism, but if there is a clarity to arrive at in such a debate, it would best patiently try to understand the politics in play, especially in terms of how the law is supposed to function in either a modern or postmodern world. "Irrationalist" could be a pejorative as well as a code word for "conservative," if both Nietzsche and Heidegger, as well as the Nazis, could be considered some sort of irrational philosophy, but nothing really about Nietzsche or Heidegger, or even the Nazis for that matter, suggested that they were purposely espousing people to appeal to an irrational side.

Still, Lyotard is the one espousing a higher aesthetic of the sublime, while Habermas's is more the aesthetic of the beautiful.[411] Simply one subtle shade of the definition of the word "sublime" versus "beautiful" allows the imagination to run away with the former as a more intense, all-encompassing emotion that can drive people to irrational behavior, while the latter is a more generic and passive representation for something that is simply pleasing or bucolic.

There really has been no direct debate between Lyotard and Habermas,[412] although there have been associates who have taken positions in the spirit of their mentors to the extent that camps have been created and battle lines drawn.[413] Lyotard does mention Habermas in *the Postmodern Condition*, and appears to quibble over Habermas's quickness to call certain French philosophers Neo-Conservatives.[414] On the other hand, if justice is a concept reflecting more the leftwing of politics, both Lyotard and Habermas share this ideal, even if Habermas's is more from an Enlightenment point of view, with Lyotard stating that justice tends to prevail in the end, but as something inevitable and not solely within the will of human beings.[415]

Certainly, both Lyotard and Habermas respect the role of intersubjectivity, or how two different personal narratives interact, finding common ground and influencing each other. What Habermas emphasizes is that through his basic building block of language, communicative action, is the ideal of finding consensus, while for Lyotard, dissensus can be as important as consensus. As a byproduct of this slightly differing norm, Lyotard welcomes a proliferation of new kinds of discourse through intersubjectivity, while Habermas tries to keep the categories of discourse well-defined and examples of discourse pure, especially scientific reason.

Lyotard's view has emphasized another aspect of postmodernism, known as agonism or agonistics. This has been championed by Mouffe,[416] but basically accepts that democracy is best an act in which all opinions, most importantly the dissenters, continue to dissent, if necessary, and not willingly accept the consensus of the majority as if any matter is once and for all resolved. For a point of contention within a democracy, this is actually an extremely fine line, in light of any rift that Habermas might have with the agonistic point of view. Still, it is now a fundamental difference between a modernist who stoically accepts the majority's opinion, if it doesn't trample upon a minority's rights, and a postmodernist who essentially threatens the process with stagnation, if a minority point of view is of such value, it deserves to be preserved. Such differences also probably reflect a certain prosperity to rest upon, while in the early days of America, the threat of survival played upon an expediency for democracy to make decisive opinions, and not to lay dormant in a deadlock of combating views.

In essence, the word "legitimation" stands for the stoic expediency approach to democracy, versus the ultimate freedom of all voices to be heard and preserved. A law is legitimated through a solemn process, and its citizens adhere to the decisions made out of respect for the process, even though they disagree with the laws. Engaging in civil disobedience once a law is enacted goes against the process of legitimation but brings with it a richer plurality of voices, which is what postmodernists intend to do.

Still, in this analysis, it is difficult to escape a simple dialectic between a democracy that solemnly expects its citizens to comply with what has been democratically decided and a democracy in which the citizens are more irreverent to the process and will to continue espousing their views, even when defeated—tomorrow is another day.

When adding to this the concept of metanarrative, the Enlightenment still stands for the creation of a grand narrative that will be the ideal that all strive for, while postmodernism allows for trial and error along the way to strengthen the ultimate plan by allowing for contingencies. Minorities transform into a majority, and vice versa. It is difficult to fathom that this simple dialectic represents a chasm, although in light of how modernism can be portrayed as an unstoppable force marching forward, even if losing its legitimacy, the cry for postmodernism to free things up is entirely reasonable.

As far as the irrational is concerned, it is difficult to allow even Habermas's criticism of postmodernism to be portrayed as postmodernists wanting to be irrational and challenging the very rationalism of the Enlightenment (let alone that this is somehow a conservative point of view and pejorative). More likely, the irrational is simply a concept that allows the rational to dip into the pool of irrationality now and then, only in search of an idea that is better suited for present circumstances. Aporia has always existed in extremes, whether humans act with utter irrationality (based on all of Habermas's observations of a society losing legitimacy in the process[417]), or whether they act with too much stoicism to the will of the majority, even when the majority has achieved its status through an artful or superior power that does not ultimately serve a democratic ideal.

By creating his own metanarrative into one book,[418] Habermas successfully sums up his philosophy of communicative action and how it has endured throughout the postmodern era, giving the project a great weight as yet another volume in the grand narrative of German philosophy. The question remains as to whether Habermas really has navigated through the postmodern era without picking up some of its ideas along the way.

Habermas succinctly puts forth Aristotle's practical reason (praktische Vernunft) as shifting from the society in ancient times to the individual during the Enlightenment. In the era of communicative action, Habermas concludes that the model has become so complex, both society and individual must be considered. By distinguishing between practical reason in the Enlightenment and what it entails now, even suggesting that the model is too complex to be pat and simple, has not Habermas constructed a model at least very similar to what postmodernists espouse?

Because the second noun in the title of Habermas's magnum opus is "validity" (Geltung), a refined concept following his earlier use of the word "legitimation,"[419] Habermas's version of postmodernism would not be the same sort of free-for-all of generally allowing all narratives to co-exist, whether part of a consensus or a separate dissensus, but only requires the extra step of validating the facts of the narrative into an enforceable law. The fact that the narrative might be part of the consensus does not automatically legitimize it, nor does the fact that it is part of the dissensus delegitimize it.

Even what has been translated into English as Habermas's word for "law," or the German word "Recht," carries with it a fairness element, unlike more common German words for "law," e.g., "Gesetz." To translate this German word into English with the more obvious word "right" has with it some different connotations, such as of our rights as understood in American law, although as a fundamental aspect of the German civil-law system, or "subjektives Recht,"[420] this word describes the fundamental aspect of legitimation that rests in the more general idea of rights as something intersubjective rather than purely atomistic to the individual.[421]

Even if lost somewhat in translation, not to mention American versus German notions of democracy and rights, the democratic process combining legitimation via rights, which have a moral element to them, and legitimation via legislation or contract, also has to it both a moral and contractual element of legitimation via consensus. Habermas is careful to allow all the nuances of several different approaches to democracy, but in these nuances blur the primacy of legitimation via consensus, if not to the same extent, at least in the same direction as the postmodernists do. The moral principal inherent in individual rights was sacred ground under the Enlightenment, or what the postmodernists might generally refer to as modernism. Compromising this sacredness with the idea that the intersubjective aspect of rights makes the idealism of the Enlightenment no longer realistic, implies that Habermas endorses a similar point of view to the postmodernists, even if he resists the comparison.

Above all, Habermas reduced the dichotomy down to human rights (Menschenrechte[422]) and popular sovereignty (Volkssouveränität[423]), but emphasized their complementary constructions. This has been further simplified to morality (Moral[424]) and law/fairness (Recht[425]). Behind both were Habermas's neutral idea of "action norms" (Handlungsnormen), summed up in the following discourse principal:

> "D: Just those action norms (Handlungsnormen) are valid ([g]ültig) to which all possible affected persons (Betroffenen) could agree as participants in rational discourses (rationalen Diskursen)."[426]

This central "discourse theory" (Diskurstheorie) of course implies that the "rational" quality of the discourse will accept both concepts. Consequently, postmodernists might be accused of many things, including following only the irrational in terms of either rejecting both concepts of morality and law, or taking sides only with the human rights side of the equation or morality.

Rebelliousness is classically such an anti-state posture that rejects its laws from a viewpoint of freedom from some sort of oppression. In modern American politics, rebelliousness has even become the new form of conservatism, in terms of not paying taxes and revolting against a liberal government.[427]

Meanwhile, classically conservative notions include a loyalty to the state, more in line with a sovereign, whether popularly derived or based on something more traditional as a bloodline or conqueror. Still, this traditional conservative has its own morality, based on these notions of loyalty, but is more a procedural type of loyalty based on positivism.

Habermas has not reinvented the wheel here, but clearly has provided nuances to go beyond traditional points of view. Two more nuances that he recognizes from 19th-century that go towards the modern political divide are "self-determination"[428] (conservative) and "self-realization"[429] (liberal). To this end, he states the following:

> "However, these ideas of self-determination and self-realization cannot be put together without tension. Not surprisingly, social-contract theories [i.e., the former] (Vernunftrecht) have responded to the modern ideals of justice (Gerechtigkeitsideen) and the good life [i.e., the latter] (Lebensideale) with answers that bear different accents."[430]

It may always be a radical stance to argue politics from the point of view that the other side of the political spectrum is always wrong. At least Habermas's discourse theory is postmodern enough to accept and even thrive off of how complementary the two sides are, even if they are not the same thing.

DIFFEREND

In comparing Habermas with Lyotard, deeper analysis allows central concepts of the two—communicative action versus differend—to clash, but also to demonstrate more similarities than either would have probably liked to have admitted back in the 1990s, when Lyotard was still alive.[431] Certainly, Lyotard freely employed his own version of Wittgenstein's language games that Habermas undoubtedly has also continued to employ, if not in a differing version involving a "rule of recognition" (Erkenntnisregel).[432]

Meanwhile, what has traditionally become the attack by critical theory of the Frankfurt School, which Habermas is often associated with, on postmodernism involves defending broad topics that postmodernism is supposed to reject, such as reason, universality, and normativity, not to mention the Enlightenment and modernity as a whole.[433] If comparing both Habermas and Lyotard can soften the sometimes exaggerated stances of the two, especially in that they share the importance of language games—Habermas as a means to find consensus through a specific and deliberate discourse theory which borrows heavily from Kant, while Lyotard is more in line with showing how the various forms of discourse as categorized by Kant (theoretical, practical, and aesthetic[434]) remain apart—finding common ground might help move beyond any perceived impasse into a new direction of thinking (hopefully a direction of thinking that can be called something other than "postpostmodernism").

What Lyotard and the postmodernists were most concerned with dealt with how minorities in a democracy can be led by the more clever factions in society to vote against their interests. Certainly Habermas's communicative action theory and struggle for consensus has hardly been characterized as condoning a sinister element to take over society with guile and misusing the process of legitimation via popular sovereignty and a resulting positivism to prevent the genuinely oppressed to free themselves from tyranny, even though real existing Communism, not to mention Fascism, have both often been accused of misusing democracy in this very way.

Such easy examples aside, what the postmodernists are mostly worried about are that minorities in democracies like the United States and modern Germany and France suffer under oppressive systems brought about by sinister elements that abuse democracy that voting people often are completely unaware of. Habermas would be more inclined to admire the process of reaching consensus in modern democracies, emphasizing the moral element in his discourse theory, which leaves open the possibility that immoral behavior can indeed cause oppression in a democracy: "Discourse theory conceives of morality as an authority that crosses the boundaries between private and public spheres (Lebensbereichen); these boundaries vary throughout history anyhow, depending on social structure (Sozialstruktur)."[435] Although such a morality might lead to a universal concept that postmodernists are popularly accused of eschewing, Habermas grounds this morality in Kant, which Lyotard has also endorsed, as the following reflection by Lyotard on Kant's notion of "presentation" (Darstellung) reveals:

> "Despite the name it bears, the Kantian *Darstellung* is not at all the presentation of a phrase universe... More generally, presentation

supposes a capacity for finding the example or the case which fits a rule, and for finding it without a rule…This capacity to judge in a nondeterminant fashion is exerted outside the realm of cognition: in morality, where just action needs to be determined with no instruction other than the moral law, which ought to leave that action undetermined…."[436]

Although Kant's idea of *Darstellung* is not limited to language, or "a phrase universe," the emphasis of morality extends to all forms of representation, including language and its interpretation.

To summarize it as simply as possible, Lyotard's concept of the differend is a situation, such as in a litigation, where both narratives cannot resolve without unjustly harming the other so that any solution favoring one side or the other will be generally unjust.[437] One can quibble as to how often such genuine situations come up in litigations or whether this is apropos of the language games that Wittgenstein was actually referring to, but at heart is the universal concept of injustice, which suggests that at least in the case of Lyotard, his postmodern stance against universal concepts as possible modes of oppression, is overstated by his critics. Whether softening the impact of the legitimation of a consensus so that all minority narratives should dutifully follow the majority as a moral act of democracy, or outright accusing a minority with an interest against the now legitimized narrative of the majority of guile and bad faith, both Lyotard and Habermas share a common ground in morality as based in Kant.[438]

In his stance towards Nietzsche, Lyotard has always been aware that among postmodernists an appeal to passion that defies all democratization and that should preserve minorities in a system of agonistics should not overstep itself. He himself quibbles about this, as the following passage from *The Differend* exemplifies:

> "[I]s postmodernity the pastime of an old man who scrounges in the garbage-heap of finality looking for leftovers, who brandishes unconsciousnesses, lapses, limits, confines, goulags, parataxes, non-senses, or paradoxes, and who turns this into the glory of his novelty, into his promise of change? But this too is a goal for a certain humanity. A genre. (A bad parody of Nietzsche. Why?)"[439]

Habermas has been especially critical of a modern French approach to Nietzsche, which he by and large attributes to Georges Bataille (1897-1962).[440] Basically, this criticism stems from a general sensitivity on

Habermas's part favoring the politically left, especially from many of the anti-Nazi currents that led Habermas to criticize Gadamer as secretly harboring authoritarian stances acquired from his mentor Heidegger.[441]

If Habermas is merely sensitive to all forms of thinking that may have at one time been instrumental in the formation of Nazi Germany and any similarities to an immoral authoritarian social theory, this alone should not prevent a final rapprochement of Habermas's communicative action and discourse theory with Lyotard's postmodernism. Marx may be a more difficult issue to resolve than Nietzsche, especially based on what remains in the West of the ruins of the Cold War, but as long as there is a moral and immoral way of conducting a democracy, implementing mechanisms to prevent the immoral would find both Habermas and Lyotard useful.

As stated in the introduction, one of the best examples of Lyotard's differend are the issues surrounding the Indian Child Welfare Act (ICWA), which in 1978 sought to prevent Indian children from being routinely removed from their cultures without necessity. Atwood deftly embraces postmodern ideals in a moderate, less caustic way to help explain the intricacies of such seemingly contradictory legal issues. Lyotard's philosophy is in this way put to practical use, as the following excerpt indicates:

> "To Lyotard, the disappearance of metanarratives has left us with the liberating potential of local, interlocking language games—a weave of intricate interconnections that has no over-arching, defining commonality. In his work, this philosopher uses the term 'differends' to mean the ways in which persons from different cultures may talk past one another because of the particular narratives and language games that are distinct to each culture."[442]

In the case of the ICWA, the policies against racism that were so instrumental in alleviating the racial unrest that typified the African American communities of America, clashed remarkably with the policies against the brutal assimilation policies that typified the ongoing struggle to preserve American Indian cultures. Ruffin's further development of the complexities of the policies behind the ICWA mentions the high suicide rate among American Indian youths as being twice the national average, and citing a sociological theory for this being that they are raised outside of their own cultural systems.[443]

Unfortunately such complexities of policy or Lyotard's differend itself have eluded one of the more recent Supreme Court decisions involving the ICWA, *Adoptive Couple v. Baby Girl*.[444] Despite the anonymity of the case's official title, this opinion provided appellants Matt and Melanie Capobianco a victory and media event which allowed them to take back custody of their once adopted daughter, Veronica, from the birth father, Dusten Brown, after the child had been in his custody for more than two years.[445] Brown's Hispanic girlfriend, Chrissy Maldonado, put the baby up for adoption, even though Brown's 3/128 Cherokee blood gave the baby 3/256 Cherokee blood, and the ICWA required that the Cherokee Nation's Tribal Court have a say in the adoption.[446]

J. Samuel Alito wrote the opinion for the majority[447] and deemed that Brown had abandoned baby Veronica at birth and therefore never had custody of her, until the South Carolina Supreme Court ruled in his favor after she was 27 months old.[448] Through an unlikely interpretation of the articulation "continued custody" as helped along by the Compact Oxford, Webster's, and American Heritage dictionaries,[449] Brown could not be eligible for the protections claimed under the ICWA because he never had "continued custody" of Veronica before the South Carolina Supreme Court granted it to him.

Aside from Alito's hermeneutical anomaly, which not even the ardent textualist J. Antonin Scalia agrees with,[450] the issue that especially gets sidestepped in *Adoptive Couple* is the clashing policies of preserving American Indian cultures on the one hand and the Equal Protection Clause of the 14th Amendment on the other. In her dissent, J. Sonia Sotomayor addresses the issue by citing notoriously controversial Federal Indian Law cases on point which bypass equal protection to protect American Indian interests.[451] Alito only mentions the Equal Protection problems briefly, but most certainly does not recognize the differend issue as such or in any such way consistent with case law Sotomayor cites.[452]

Adoptive Couple was a case that involved high emotions from both sides, although it is not clear in the media blitz how the legal theories were playing out as they were upstaged by the emotional heartstrings created from a baby girl born in Oklahoma, raised for the first two years in South Carolina by an adoptive couple, moved back to Oklahoma to be raised by her birth father for the next two years of her life, and then finally moved back to the adoptive couple permanently. Watching the potent policy arguments from both sides ostensibly overlooked the fact that the baby girl was only 3/256 Cherokee, on the one hand, and will probably have more emotional trauma being taken away from her birth father at age four than the previous removal from adoptive parents at age two. Meanwhile, the original policy of ICWA becomes gutted substantially by the ruling, but above all, the differend aspect of Equal Protection policy versus permitted Federal racial classifications for American Indians is completely ignored, with the exception of its being mentioned in the dissent by Sotomayor.

Whatever the ultimate political dynamics of *Adoptive Couple* are, the side that might end up favoring Lyotard's postmodernism did not prevail. Whether sending out conservative messages to unwed couples and deadbeat dads that the Court favors more stable households for raising children, or even the more pernicious message of preferring a white upbringing for an innocent baby to an American Indian upbringing, if there's actually a choice to be made, such a timely and sensationalized Supreme Court case demonstrates that there is nothing particularly settled when it comes to reforming the American legal system to comport to the ongoing postmodern dialogue. Although this is only one example, the implication is that American politics may still consider such Continental European legal philosophies as Lyotard's with suspicion. Postmodernism may therefore not be abandoned entirely as passé, but, rather, something to be refined and perfected into a new cycle of argumentation.

CHAPTER FOUR

ANALYSIS AND CONCLUSION

Efforts to "reclaim history"[453] at the beginning of the 21st centu-
ry are producing sanitized stories generously borrowing from old
American myths that were once widely thought to be moribund
and no longer plausible.[454] Perhaps this reclamation especially inspired
the one fell swoop through a jurisdictional maze in which Aquash, once
believed to be a legendary victim of the same right-wing extremism she
dedicated her life to fighting, became a victim of left-wing militant radi-
calism.

If the original notion is correct and members of GOONs killed her, it
probably happened somewhere other than where her body was dumped,
and the FBI initially did nothing. Looking Cloud said he took the gun
from Graham after the execution of Aquash and fired the remaining bullets into the ground. No such bullets or bullet holes in the ground were
ever found at the location identified by Looking Cloud as the murder site
(i.e., near the cliff her body was thrown over).

It's also unlikely that feisty Aquash would have ever allowed a lower
level AIM operative such as Theda Clarke to "arrest" her, let alone to tie
her to a board and transport her as a prisoner in the back of a Pinto hatchback. The large rear window of a Pinto hatchback would have allowed any
motorist between Colorado and South Dakota to see a woman tied up inside. Witnesses who claimed to see Aquash restrained this way at Clarke's
residence could have easily been tricked by innuendo, coaching, or some
other theatrics.

Graham's early version of events has him driving Aquash and Looking Cloud to the Pine Ridge Reservation without Clarke or even Clarke's
knowledge. No one was tied up, and Aquash was dropped off at a friend's
house at her request. He has changed his story substantially.

Aside from a nagging embarrassment that the FBI went through trying
to deny that anything was known about Aquash's murder, legal machi-

nations and outright depredations surrounding the Peltier trial induced even more anti-FBI sentiments. A new mop-up of the Aquash case allowed a convenient way to push back on the growing popular sentiment for Peltier.

Peltier claims he did little else than blindly fire his rifle at a distance from the gun battle that ensued between Agents Coler and Williams and three other AIM members: Bob Robideau, Norman Charles, and Joe Stuntz (who also perished). Robideau, who seems to have originated the cover story that a red pickup truck was involved, admits he fired the shot that would have caused Coler to bleed out. Even though Robideau was acquitted on a self-defense theory and protected by his right against double jeopardy, he never confessed publicly and did not testify at Peltier's trial to being the one who committed the close range executions of the agents.

After these ignoble deaths of Coler and Williams, the frustrated FBI instinctively went after the three most prominent and most wanted AIM members: Robideau, Butler, and Peltier. As much as this might have been perceived as at least overkill, it probably did include the man who most likely committed the executions, Robideau.

Just the same, even the close range executions should have been more vigorously analyzed according to theories of adequate provocation, which would have amounted to voluntary manslaughter for Robideau rather than murder. His acts no doubt proceeded while in a panic state following the death of his colleague Stuntz. Even defense attorney William Kunstler appeared a bit shocked that a self-defense theory for Robideau and Butler based on the martial law declared on the reservation could prevail.

As a heroin addict, Looking Cloud still has memories of his 1975 trip to South Dakota with Canadians Graham and Aquash, serving as their guide to the reservation he grew up on. Should we really not dare to suspect that Looking Cloud's close "blood brother," Richard Two Elk, who wrote the foreword to the FBI's new myth of the events,[455] coached a few extra facts into Looking Cloud's already foggy memory? In fact, perhaps the revelations from Looking Cloud, whose arrangement with the FBI yielded him a life sentence in prison, might be an artfully induced piece of pure fiction, based on only dribs and drabs of innocuous fact. Different juries did not dare question Looking Cloud's narrative as presented to them, but legal postmodernists may acknowledge the procedure the jury verdicts created and still wonder about an actual truth or injustice that might warrant clemency from the President.

In this way, the implausibility of Looking Cloud's ultimate narrative and its legitimation also suggest that despite its many safeguards and painstaking care in procedure, the legal system encountered a situation that has morphed into a genuine differend, according to Lyotard's definition. In other words, when such argumentation depends on such suspicious narratives that are nonetheless legitimatized, the law itself should acknowledge the conundrum it has encountered and singlehandedly created.

Aside from its language games, aporia, and blatant contradictions, postmodernism stands for a softening of modernity through the lens of the Enlightenment. Narrative, legitimation, and differend as defined in the previous chapter and now illustrated with the Aquash and Peltier cases can thus form a three-prong test for seemingly contradictory, postmodern legal situations. If these three concepts promulgated three simple standards (1. don't oppress minority narratives; 2. allow democratically prevailing narratives their procedural legitimation, but without undue oppression of rights; and 3. recognize and respect a differend when encountered by finding an alternative solution between the two disputing narratives without declaring winner and loser), postmodernism could be policy inserted somewhere into a Supreme Court decision or written up somehow as the preamble of a bill by Congress.

On the other hand, postmodernism as an era of Western philosophy is typically expounded not with a voice of friendly persuasion, but as the necessary new modernity. This appears to be inescapable as a rule of advocacy. In other words, it must be followed, the adherents typically say. Its appeal to morality, especially through Kant, is like any such appeal: humanity and civilization require of us to adopt postmodernism to protect minority narratives from oppression and to insure that language games do not accumulate into an inescapable conundrum.

Stated in such terms, it remains, like so many other language games, something with no logical conclusion. A boundary of ignorance typically protects partakers of discourse and argumentation from getting too close to the sheer terror that language can inevitably never resolve itself or anything. To mutually agree not to cross unstated but clear boundaries simplifies the reality of both sides to an argument, until the brutality of injustice sets in and forces a losing side to not accept the other side's victory by any means possible.

Legal postmodernism as a critique of the fundamental flaw of democracy (oppression by the majority), often also gives rise to outright anti-democratic points of view with someone like Machiavelli or Nietzsche as a muse. Counterintuitively, it often emerges on the politically left side of things. Clearly, some not only do not want the softening to occur, but would rather see society move to even more rigid standards. Perhaps this defines the recognition of postmodernism as a politically left concept against the more objective attempt by the political right to rid language of its games once and for all. So how should the right side of things view postmodernism?

Tom Sawyer's great prank of getting out of his punishment for fighting by convincing his friends that whitewashing the fence is such a great pastime that he will only allow them to do it if they give him something of value in exchange, makes for a charming argument in favor of the free use of guile in capitalism.[456] Postmodern arguments that such guile should be looked upon as the creation of oppression tell a markedly different narrative as to how democracy should proceed, since ultimately what Tom and his friends have created is a unanimous consensus, despite what a skeptical onlooker might feel about the arrangement. Likewise, the guileful Wizard of Oz has little guilt in spreading the mythic narrative that a powerfully magic force rules over the great city making its inhabitants fear something that does not exist, because after all, he is not a bad man, but simply a "bad wizard."[457]

To dismiss postmodernists simply for being too persnickety or having no sense of humor in assessing the ways of the world, or dismissing the agonistics suffered by the minorities of a democracy as nothing more unjust than hard knock lessons, is in line with an ideologically competitive society like the United States. The aggressive tenets of capitalism have certainly marched on throughout the postmodern era since 1975, even though collapses in the free market system roughly every decade (S&L crisis that finally ceased in 1995; Enron Scandal of 2001; and the subprime mortgage collapse of 2008) all accompanied by major Government bailouts, ought to have cast some light on the idea of safeguarding a purely free market with some oversights and safety measures. Even in a hypothetical situation where the majority has ultimately been tricked into something against their interests, as well as the interests of the minorities, finding anything wrong with the deception may prove a hard sell in such a historical context.

Moreover, the injustice finally felt by those tricked into forming an illusory majority (i.e., when they finally form a different face to the deception in their own mind that has fooled them) makes for just as much instability in a democracy which uses legitimation as a mere loophole to some more sinister, selfish end than any other base tyranny found in history from ancient times onward. Harry Truman famously made political hay of this sentiment during his 1948 Presidential reelection campaign with the saying, "How many times do you have to be hit over the head before you figure out who's hitting you,"[458] but such once common overt suspicion of being fooled in a democracy often gives way to the comfort of safety, as long as the voter in a democracy believes they are included among the ranks of the good people being protected.

For all these good reasons, at least Lyotard's differend should never be something that a healthy democracy ignores, because the phenomenon is so easy to demonstrate, with the Aquash and Peltier cases serving as only two out of many prime examples of how contradicting policies make a mess of things. There is a strong tendency in a democracy and its legal disputes in courts to treat disputes as cosmic forces and that nature will select its champions, much like the Roman tradition of *litiscontestatio*, or trial by ordeal[459] or the laissez faire capitalist who believes that natural selection fairly chooses what ought to be preserved and what is not worth preserving.

This concept has won remarkable popular sway during the last quarter of the 20th-century, despite its profound metaphysical implications within what can be a brutally rigid doctrine of the Chicago School of Economics or Libertarianism.[460] If you belong to one of the narratives that nature has chosen for extinction, the brutality can especially be experienced, as well as the notion that a modern dogma has prevailed.

As for juries in a litigation, a similar type of deference to a unanimous verdict is so sacred that it is rarely skeptically questioned without good cause during the appellate process. The legal system's desperate need for certainty finds it in how laypeople decide an issue—a sacred process not to be disturbed unless absolutely necessary.

The previous chapter began by relating humble origins of the word "postmodern" from architecture and music, as well as flamboyant literary criticism.[461] These are still relevant to postmodern social and philosophical theories, if not the best and purest source to help illustrate such theories, inasmuch as democracy and law should not idealize the mechanical (architecture) and not prohibit narratives based on a purist assumption that to every era, one "true" narrative will prevail which is newer and more improved than the era preceding it (music). Postmodernism does not discard legitimation altogether, but can find consensus by majority (if not by outright unanimity) useful as a fallible, intersubjective communicative action, but not as the sacred infallible ritual it is recognized as still today.

If the humblest of origins give us a glimpse of postmodernism in its simplest form—modernism representing a sort of social rigidity and postmodernism softening that—we are left with not much more than a political stance relevant only within its historical context. Clearly postmodernism prevailed in forms such as the United Nations, as well as freeing up the arts from an esoteric purism by acceptance of more popular forms of art and music. Postmodernism did not prevail in all the ways Neo-Conservatism prevailed since 1975: capitalism as an ideology, renewed reliance on the military and defense, and a return to fundamental Christianity.

The burning question that remains at this point is to what extent will postmodernism be relevant now and into the near future? Has the purity that the Enlightenment represented through the need for metanarrative been supplanted with more tolerance for differing, minority views? What will the role of language games continue to play?

Without excessive soothsaying, the term "postmodernism" has probably outplayed its usefulness, based on more than anything the way it has satisfactorily reached its own consensus as to what it is. By its own definition, it should now yield its own sort of metanarrative to other more relevant and controversial narratives.

Modern law almost always carries with it a proviso that the appearance of politics in voluble legal opinions is illusion. Of course, that is not so. Our legal system is adversarial by definition, and therefore, zealous advocacy requires that legal actors never break character, even down to the last appeal by the lowest single litigant.

In fact, our American legal system suffers greatly from politicization disguised as complex legal analysis. The principle of reliance on impenetrable gobbledygook to protect the layperson who normally can't understand it also brings with it one of the purest forms of fakery that heated political discussions can be fueled by.

As a politically potent controversy with power to be a provocative force in any dialogue about the relevancy of new ideas, postmodernism no longer packs the same punch. When Fukuyama declared the "end of history" with the falling of the Berlin Wall,[462] the statement appeared to even respected intellectuals and commentators to make no sense, so much so that postmodernism was its own voluntary laughing stock. The previous year, the author even recalls his own experience with the controversy that the word could create when interviewing composer John Cage who was appearing in a postmodern symposium.[463] Only days later, a memorandum circulated at the otherwise respected and powerful newspaper the author was employed at banning the word "postmodernism" in all future stories—and this was one of Cage's few moments where he was actually vehemently against a new trend in music.[464]

Clearly, the language games can still be the source of much controversy, although somehow the 20th-century will always be the time when language, math, and science all became something of a mystery again. That particular initial shock of returning to a sense of unreliability in the universe will no doubt upstage any subsequent shock.

That leaves the issue of law, which naturally is bound closely to politics and a theory of society in general. Lyotard also spent much of his postmodernism theories on how technology and computers facilitate the thinking.[465] This aspect of postmodernism has now surpassed all expectations from the 1970s with the Internet, offering a free flow of narratives from all over the world and different political points of view. An encyclopedia known as Wikipedia appears to be functioning in a useful way, even without a ruthless process of legitimation that a powerful editor provides.

The law has also succumbed to the modern pressures of the Internet and forms of alternative dispute resolution. Together with the still thriving laissez faire capitalism that has driven the decades of postmodernism, the United States stands closer than ever to actually privatizing the law, which undoubtedly would limit access to it for all but the most wealthy. Even Habermas dared not speculate about a future that did not include democracy, but privatization has its own inevitable side effects, such as legitimation that probably would eventually go to the highest bidder instead of any attempt at a consensus (if many things do not work that way already in the United States and around the world).

If Lyotard's differend remains a useful topic in such a context, there would need to be a renewal of the importance of democracy, perhaps even a "neo-democracy," that would provide a rigorous critique of how democracies have evolved up to now, and especially the real existing differend in America between a runaway capitalism that creates its own new dynasties of royal blood and the stubborn notion of democracy which appears to preserve "one man one vote" and other "fair" forms of consensus, such as a unanimous jury.

Still, before such a neo-democracy movement could be effective, it would probably have to withstand the last moments of a harsh winter. In order to weather such a winter, crawling inside the carcass of a dead

91

postmodernism might help keep any newer, better ideas warm. Postmodernism would have to indeed be dead for that to happen.

If likewise summing up the topic of legal hermeneutics in order to put an end to it were possible to do in a conclusive way, it would no doubt begin with the broad claim that the topic is nothing but simply an ongoing affirmation of ancient ideals. This would lead to its own form of "vicious circle" in that hermeneuts are actually originalists, but also that originalists are also hermeneuts. But most of all, it affirms the living nature of texts and their meaning in a way antithetical to Scalia's way along with his fellow conservatives.

That is not to say, on the other hand, that the modern practice of textualism and originalism should be free to practice their own form of hermeneutics based on cutting a tether from past to present. Renewing the process of legal hermeneutics via Gadamer hopefully reinforced the idea that the tether between a law written in the past must keep its relevance to living people, and that interpretation based on phronesis is really the only way that a constitution such as America's, written over 200 years ago, can still remain relevant and serve all of the purposes that law should and could possibly serve.

If the ongoing practice of what has been called all along legal hermeneutics in American common law demonstrates something provocative, it is that heckling goes both ways, as the sarcasm of the California criminal courts has put down in the record, as well as the challenge in the previous chapter to Scalia's interpretation of "cruel and unusual." The aporia here may suggest that hermeneutics should remain what it has been (perhaps something based more on Lieber's version of it), and not to be an instrument that engages in a political impasse that might have several issues such as abortion, segregation, and use of the death penalty, attached to it.

Still, this has not been the case and probably should not be the case. The advocates of legal hermeneutics have become highly political, and it would be a mistake to disregard any political underpinnings in the Gadamer-Habermas debate, even suggesting the tumultuous political currents of Germany between the wars.

When placed into the American political arena, the powerful Neo-Conservative movement strengthened their hand in the 1970s when they dared take the Anarchy card away from the American left and put in in their own hand. They did this under the highly intellectual veil of Libertarianism, as culminating in the title of modern Libertarian Ron Paul's book, *End the Fed*.[466]

In context of George Washington's "original intent" of initiating a unified Federal government in 1789 that would never fall prey to political parties or factionalism, it is still nearly impossible to conclusively pinpoint what might be the ultimate political dialogue in modern American politics were it to be simplified between originalism on one side and legal hermeneutics on the other. On the one hand it might be as simple as to say one side wants to end Democratic government and the other side wants to preserve it, even if stretches of time find liberals and conservatives alternating between these two extremes. It might be even something more nuanced, such as the cartoonish debates between Daddy Warbucks and FDR in the musical *Annie*.[467]

In the end, Ricœur's two-part formulations—of alienation versus belonging, or suspicion versus faith—makes for perhaps an affirmation of George Washington's position that both sides of any issue should co-exist in a complementary way. Unfortunately this also once again confronts the fallacy of false equivalence, not to mention Lyotard's differend.

If legal hermeneutics accomplishes anything, it is something ambient that is the common law's built-in safety net. To use it to drive a stake through the heart of textualism or originalism might have its own petty political motivations, but will always espouse something living and human over a text on the page that we should assume died hundreds of years ago.

Endnotes

1   Timothy Williams, New Inquiry of Deaths on Reservation in the 1970s, *N.Y. Times* (June 19, 2012), available at http://www.nytimes.com/2012/06/20/us/new-inquiry-of-deaths-on-reservation-in-the-1970s.html?_r=0 (published only weeks after new conclusions in John Graham's litigations in South Dakota). See *United States v. Graham*, 2012 S.D. 42, 815 N.W.2d 293 (2012) (hereinafter Graham III).

2   Id.On the other hand, many independent observers suggest this number is closer to 200.

3   Id.

4   Peter Matthiessen, *In the Spirit of Crazy Horse* 110 (Penguin Books 1992) (1983).

5   Id. at 256.

6   Id.at 146.

7   Id. at xx.

8   Nitel from FBI Rapid City Office, to Director and all offices via Wash. HQ, FBI, Mar. 15, 1976, 6:50 P.M., ANNA MAE AQUASH, AKA (DECEASED), -VICTIM, CIR - MURDER, Bureau File RC 70-11023, in Antoinette Nora Claypoole ed., Ghost Rider Roads: the American Indian Movement 471-74 (2d ed. 2013).

9   Matthiessen, supra note 4, at 572-73.

10   Graham III, 815 N.W.2d at 297. Cf. Matthiessen, supra note 4, at 146. See also Justice for Anna Mae and Ray, http://www.jfamr.org (last visited Aug. 1, 2022); and infra note 214.

11   The two "foot soldiers," Fritz Arlo Looking Cloud and John "John Boy Patton" Graham, have by now been convicted for crimes based on Aquash's death, as related in the following trial and four published opinions on this crime: *United States v. Looking Cloud*, CR 03-50020 (D.S.D. Apr. 23, 2004) (hereinafter Looking Cloud I), trial tr. available at Justice for Anna Mae and Ray, supra note 10, https://www.jfamr.org/doc/ (last visited Aug. 1, 2022); *United States v. Looking Cloud*, 419 F.3d 781 (8th Cir. 2005) (hereinafter Looking Cloud II); *United States v. Graham*, 585 F.Supp.2d 1144 (D.S.D. 2008) (hereinafter Graham I); *United States v. Graham*, 572 F.3d 954 (8th Cir. 2009) (hereinafter Graham II), reh'g denied and reh'g en banc denied, 598 F.3d. 930 (8th Cir. 2009); and Graham III, supra note 1.

12   After John Adams's "government of laws, and not of men." See David Luban, Natural Law as Professional Ethics: A Reading of Fuller, *Natural Law and Modern Moral Philosophy*, Vol. 18, Social Philosophy and Policy, Part 1, 176 n.2 (2001).

13   See Aristotle, *Nicomachean Ethics* bk. V, at 18 (G.P. Goold ed., H. Rackham trans., Harvard Univ. Press rev. ed. 1934) (c. 384 B.C.E.).

14   See Antonin Scalia, *A Matter of Interpretation* 23-25 (1997).

15   The original *Wahrheit und Methode* (1960) has appeared in several revised German versions, while the first 1975 translation into English by an English publisher, Sheed & Ward, used the second German revision of 1965 as its source, without specific reference to who translated it. A revised second English edition in 1989 and another English version in 2004 were translated by Joel Weinsheimer and Donald G. Marshall; this research uses the following: Hans-Georg Gadamer, Wahrheit und Methode: Grundzüge einer philosophischen Hermeneutik (Mohr 4th ed. 1975) (1960).

16   See generally Ayn Rand, *Atlas Shrugged* (1957) (culminating in a famous radio broadcast by the protagonist, John Galt, who is spokesman for a group of elites that withdraws from society, believing it has oppressed them with governing ideals of equality).

17   Cf. Jack Matlock, Jr., *Reagan and Gorbachev: How the Cold War Ended* (2004).

18   Roe v. Wade, 410 U.S. 113 (1973); overruled by *Dobbs v. Jackson Women's Health Organization*, 597 U.S. ___ (2022).

19   *Brown v. Board of Education*, 347 U.S. 483 (1954). Warren's gift for getting a unanimous decision at the behest of a concerned executive would be taped a decade later in the Warren Report.

20   See Raoul Berger, *Government By Judiciary: The Transformation of the Fourteenth Amendment* (1977) (attacking the legal theories behind what its author perceives as the Warren Court's

improper expansion of "equal protection" and "due process").

21   See generally Robert H. Bork, Neutral Principals and Some First Amendment Problems, 47 Ind. L.J. 1 (1971) (advocating a "Madisonian" approach to jurisprudence that requires judges to be neutral to the intentions of the Founding Fathers, especially criticizing the Warren Court); see also Robert H. Bork, The Tempting of America: The Political Seduction of the Law 75-76 (1990) (attacking further the Warren Court with desegregated schools being outside the purview of the Founding Fathers' intent).

22   Cf. Scalia, supra note 14, at 41-44.

23   See generally David Couzens Hoy, *The Critical Circle: Literature and History in Contemporary Hermeneutics* (1978).

24   See e.g. John T. Valauri, *As Time Goes By: Hermeneutics and Originalism*, 10 Nev. L.J. 719 (2010) (examining new applications of the Gadamerian concepts of "application" and "practical wisdom," as well as "legal hermeneutics").

25   See e.g. Gyburg Radke-Uhlmann, ed., Phronesis: Die Tugend der Geisteswissenschaften (2012) (extracting the concept of "phronesis" to a central concept in the humanities).

26   See *United States v. Windsor*, 570 U.S. 744 (2013) (overturning the Defense of Marriage Act).

27   Matthiessen, supra note 4, at 256. Other versions of the discovery of the body and autopsy vary to some degree in details. See Johanna Brand, *The Life and Death of Anna Mae Aquash 13 (1993)*.

28   Testimony of Rodger Amiotte, Looking Cloud I, supra note 11, http://www.jfamr.org/doc /amiotte.html (last visited Aug. 1, 2022). Cf. Testimony of Nate Merrik, id., http://www.jfamr.org/doc/merrick.html (last visited Aug. 1, 2022) (stating the body was 60 to 70 yards west of the highway at the bottom of an 18-foot ravine).

29   Matthiessen, supra note 4, at xvi.

30   Id. at 256.

31   Id.

32   Id. at 259-60; and Nate Merrick Testimony, Looking Cloud I, supra note 28.

33   Id. at 257.

34   Id.

35   Id.

36   Id. A recent account by an FBI agent at the time strenuously attempts to shed a different light on the confusion over these events than Matthiessen does. Joseph H. Trimbach, American Indian Mafia (2009).

37   Graham II, 572 F.3d at 954.

38   Major Crimes Act, 18 U.S.C. § 1153 (2006) (requiring Federal jurisdiction for specific crimes by an Indian against "another Indian or another person").

39   18 U.S.C. § 2 (2006).

40   18 U.S.C. § 1111 (2006).

41   Graham II, 572 F.3d at 954; see infra note 45.

42   Antoinette Nora Claypoole, Notes from first KPFK broadcast, in Ghost Rider Roads 175, supra note 8.

43   Sometimes her name is spelled "Clark" in official documents. She was never indicted for the murder of Aquash, presumably because she was unfit for trial, suffering from dementia. See Andrea J. Cook, Former AIM Activist Connected to Aquash Case Dies at 87, Rapid City Journal (Oct. 12, 2011, 5 A.M.), available at http://rapidcityjournal.com/news/former-aim-activist-connected-to-aquash-case-dies-at/article6032f8fa-f47a-11e0-9d58-001cc4c03286.html. Peltier's former lawyer claims there was not good reason not to indict Clarke, and she was declared competent at the trial of Marshall and Graham in 2010. E-mail from Barry Bachrach, former attorney for Leonard Peltier, to author (Mar. 31, 2013, 8:55 AM) (on file with the author).

44   Looking Cloud II, 419 F.3d at 790.

45   Testimony of Troy Lynn Yellow Wood, Looking Cloud I, supra note 11, http://www.jfamr.

org /doc/troytest.html (last visited Aug. 1, 2022). FBI reports indicate Aquash herself organized the meeting to raise money for Peltier's bond. Cover Page from FBI Rapid City Office, William B. Wood of FBI, C, May 6, 1977, UNSUB; ANNA MAE QAUASH, aka (DECEASED) – VICTIM, Bureau File RC 70-11023, in Ghost Rider Roads 482, supra note 8.

46   Looking Cloud II, 419 F.3d at 790 (relating that Aquash had actually been tied to a board at this time and was unable to walk on her own). Testimony of Angie Janis, Looking Cloud I, supra note 11, http://www.jfamr.org/doc/janis.html (last visited Aug. 1, 2022) (describing a romantic relationship between Janis and Graham, and that Aquash was tied to a board, even though no other witness provided this detail). Cf. Yellow Wood Testimony, supra note 30 (describing Aquash as getting into the Pinto with Clarke and the others, but never saw her hands tied). Cf. interview by Claypoole of Graham (Mar. 30, 2004), in Ghost Rider Roads 507, supra note 8 (claiming that Aquash alone approached Graham to drive her from Denver to Rapid City, and although they used Clarke's Pinto for the trip, Clarke did not go along for the ride).

47   There is no mention in Looking Cloud II about them spending the rest of the night in Rapid City, although this would have been at the house of Thelma Rios who was not home, but who negotiated a guilty plea for accessory to kidnapping Nov. 8, 2010, for this minor role in the Aquash murder, but also for making telephone calls faciltating Aquash's "arrest," and was sentenced to five years in prison, with the sentence constructively commuted to probation. Press Release, Marty J. Jackley, Attorney General of South Dakota, Thelma Rios Enters Plea in 1975 Aquash Case (Nov. 8, 2010), available at http://atg.sd.gov/News/NewsReleases/NewsReleasesView/tabid/441/itemID/2581/moduleID/597/Default.aspx. Cf. Mary Garrigan, Rios, Accessory in Aquash murder, dead at 65, Rapid City Journal (Feb. 11, 2011, 6:30 A.M.), available at http://rapidcityjournal.com/news/rios-accessory-in-aquash-murder-dead-at/article_520e1afc-3580-11e0-9546-001cc4c002e0.html.

48   Testimony of Candy Hamilton, Looking Cloud I, supra note 11, http://www.jfamr.org/doc /candy.html (last visited Aug. 1, 2022). Cf. Graham III, 815 N.W.2d at 306 (acknowledging that for the Graham trial, Hamilton changed her story so that this meeting at WKLD/OC took place on Dec. 15, three days after the Dec. 12 date set in Looking Cloud I as the day Aquash was murdered).

49   Graham III, 815 N.W.2d at 307 (stating that they arrived with a bound Aquash at Marshall's house in Allen at 10:30 P.M.); Marshall was indicted but acquitted of having a role in the Aquash murder. Heidi Bell Gease, Richard Marshall found not guilty in 1975 AIM slaying, Rapid City Journal (Apr. 23, 2010, 6:30 AM), available at http://rapidcityjournal.com/news/richard-marshall-found-not-guilty-in-aim-slaying /article_ef7b952c-4e30-11df-a36b-001cc4c03286.html (suggesting as well that Marshall supplied them with the gun that eventually killed Aquash).

50   Looking Cloud does not remember stopping here in the only official record of his story, a taped interview. Interview by Robert Ecoffey of Fritz Arlo Looking Cloud (Mar. 27, 2003), supra note 11, http://www.jfamr.org/doc/ecoffey2.html (last visited Aug. 1, 2022); and Bachrach E-mail, supra note 43.

51   Looking Cloud II, 419 F.3d at 790 (describing testimony from Looking Cloud's friend Richard Two Elk that Looking Cloud actually gave the gun to Graham and nodded, the only evidence that Looking Cloud aided and abetted in this crime).

52   Looking Cloud Interview, supra note 35. Cf. Testimony of William Wood, Looking Cloud I, supra note 11, http://www.jfamr.org/doc/wood.html (last visited Aug. 1, 2022) (stating that FBI searches of the area with a metal detector after the second autopsy failed to find either spent casings or bullets fired into the ground). See supra note 45.

53   Looking Cloud Interview, supra note 50.

54   Looking Cloud II, 419 F.3d at 784.

55   Id.

56   Graham III, 815 N.W.2d at 296.

57   Graham II, 572 F.2d at 954.

58   Id.; Graham I, 585 F.Supp.2d at 1148.

59   See Major Crimes Act, supra note 38.

60   Originally stemming from the Trade and Intercourse Act of July 22, 1790 § 5, Chap. XXXIII, 1 Stat. 137, and the Act of Mar. 3, 1817, ch. 92, 3 Stat. 383, the Indian Country Crimes Act (§

1152) preceded the Major Crimes Act (§ 1153) by several decades. Three cases known as the "Mc-Bratney trilogy" have since limited § 1152 to strictly "interracial" (see infra note 67) crimes: *United States v. McBratney*, 104 U.S. 621 (1881) (holding that once Colorado became a state, there was no longer Federal jurisdiction for a crime involving non-Indians on the Ute Reservation according to the "equal footing" doctrine); *Draper v. United States*, 164 U.S. 240 (1896) (holding that when Montana became a state, language in the enabling act did not prevent the new state of establishing jurisdiction over a crime involving two "negroes" on the Crow Indian Reservation); and New York ex rel. Ray v. Martin, 326 U.S. 496 (1948) (applying McBratney to a habeas corpus proceeding involving a murder between two non-Indians in the City of Salamanca, part of the Allegheny Reservation of the Seneca Tribe).

61   Graham II, 572 F.3d at 954-55. Federal charges were dismissed without prejudice. See infra note 65.

62   Graham III, 815 N.W.2d at 296, n. 1 (citing the now-defunct version of the South Dakota felony-murder statute that would have been in power, S.D. Codified Laws § 22-16-9, but which had already been repealed by SL 2005, ch 120, § 158, Jul. 1, 2006). Id. at 300, n. 6 (mentioning again this old statute along with kidnapping and felony murder, S.D. Codified Laws § 22-19-1, and premeditated murder, S.D. Codified Laws § 22-16-4); a third state charge of murder as the result of rape was dropped.

63   Id. at 297.

64   Id. at 308. See supra note 1.

65   E-mail from John R. Murphy, former attorney for John Graham, to author (May 30, 2013, 3:20 PM) (on file with author).

66   Robert N. Clinton, *Criminal Jurisdiction over Indian Lands: A Journey Through a Jurisdictional Maze*, 18 Ariz. L. Rev. 503 (1976).

67   Id. at 527 (discussing how the McBratney trilogy (see supra note 60) also created a common law bright-line rule for "interracial crimes," which were defined only as crimes with a single victim and single perpetrator where one or the other, but not both, is Indian and the crime takes place on Indian Territory; on the other hand, the McBratney trilogy did not account for using § 1152 for crimes with multiple defendants and/or victims). Only Looking Cloud was an "Indian" (Lakota Sioux) for these purposes.

68   Graham II, 572 F.3d at 954-55.

69   Conspiracy is not one of the enumerated crimes in the Major Crimes Act, supra note 38.

70   *McCormick v. Kopmann*, 161 N.E.2d 720, 727 (Ill. Ct. App. 1959) (holding that "sound policy" allows different theories of an event to be pleaded simultaneously).

71   United States' Mem. in Opp'n to Def.'s Mot. to Dismiss Indictment at 6-11, Graham I (D.S.D. Sep. 30, 2008) (No. 5:03-cr-50020-LLP); available at 2008 WL 4533613.

72   Graham I, 585 F.Supp.2d at 1148 (emphasizing that aiding and abetting is necessarily linked to an "underlying substantive offense," such as murder, and therefore cannot stand alone).

73   Id. The court cites *United States v. Williams*, 429 F.3d 767, 775 (8th Cir. 2005) (holding that because there is a Federal right to a grand jury, any missing element on the face of an indictment would probably not have been considered by the grand jury, in essence violating of the 5th Amendment).

74   Graham II, 572 F.3d at 955. In a confusing twist, the opinion states that "[t]he court dismissed Count III, preserving Counts I and II for trial," id., although the opinion does not mention that these preserved counts only applied to Marshall, who was being tried together with Graham. Murphy E-mail, supra note 65. This still does not account for why the second count, for Aquash's Indian identity, had to be also preserved as the proceedings against Marshall continued.

75   Graham had already waived his right to a speedy trial, based on the voluminous amounts of evidence that was presented to him by the prosecution and the time required to sort through it all, Carson Walker, Defendant in AIM Wants Delay of Three Months, *Rocky Mtn. News* (Mar. 5, 2008), available at 2008 WLNR 4366960. For jeopardy to attach at the Federal level, the jury had to be empaneled and sworn, which constant delays in starting the trial prevented. *Crist v. Bretz*, 437 U.S. 28, 29 (1978). According to Graham's attorney, the jury was never empanelled. Murphy E-mail, supra note 50. Therefore, the doctrine of duel sovereignty which allowed the state court to take

over, Abbate v. United States, 359 U.S. 187, 196 (1959), and presumably would not have prevented a tribal court to take over as well, *United States v. Wheeler*, 435 U.S. 313, 332 (1978), would allow the Federal court to take over again, were Graham able to have a writ of habeas corpus issued, Murphy E-mail, supra note 50, and the Indian identity issues could again be raised. The district court made clear that the dismissal of the indictments against Graham was made "without prejudice" and the "right to reindict and reprosecute" was preserved. Graham I, 585 F.Supp.2d at 1148. See supra, note 61.

76   Graham II, 572 F.3d at 957.

77   The state jurisdiction theory was based on the fact that in driving Aquash through Pennington County, South Dakota, that was not part of any Indian reservation, part of the kidnapping which led to the murder took place off of Indian Territory. Murphy E-mail, supra note 65.

78   Oddly enough, commentary for a proposed "Indian identity" statute which would have been titled "18 U.S.C. § 1150" specifically addressed and solved the issue of Canadian and Mexican Indians in United States Federal courts. Clinton, see supra note 50, at 513-14, n. 48; in the United States' Mem., supra note 71, a case was found from a Court of Appeals in Washington that stated "…the United States recognizes the racial statute of Canadian Indians…." *United States v. Daniels*, 16 P.3d 650, 654 (Wash. Ct. App. 2001), cited in United States Mem., supra note 71, at 6-7.

79   This canon of statutes and cases includes the Trade and Intercourse Act of 1834 § 25, 4 Stat. 733, 25 U.S.C. 217 (repealed 1948); *United States v. Antelope*, 430 U.S. 641, 645 (1895) (determining that racial classifications in Federal legislation regarding Indians is not impermissible and does not violate equal protection); and Westmoreland v. United States, 155 U.S. 545, 547 (1895) (clarifying that if the indictment declares that defendants are not Indians committing a crime on Indian territory, that is sufficient clarify jurisdiction).

80   *United States v. Torres*, 733 F.2d 449, 454 (7th Cir. 1984) (holding that under § 1152 Indian aspects of charge or necessary elements of the crime); United States v. Pemberton, 405 F.3d 656, 659 (8th Cir. 2005) (confirming that Indian status is a necessary element under § 1153).

81   In re Winship, 397 U.S. 358, 368 (1970) (establishing a right to reasonable doubt standard).

82   Fed. R. Civ. P. 12(b)(1).

83   Pemberton, 405 F.3d at 659; see supra note 80; and *United States v. White Horse*, 316 F.3d 769, 772 (8th Cir. 2003) (holding that when an Indian does not raise his status during trial where the victim is Indian, the complementary nature of §§ 1152 and 1153 does not create a fatal error).

84   *United States v. Norquay*, 905 F.2d 1157, 1162 (8th Cir. 1990) (holding that a non-Indian accomplice must be tried in state court).

85   Id.

86   Murphy E-mail, supra note 65.

87   *Pennoyer v. Neff*, 95 U.S. 714, 724 (1877) (stating that service of process to the person physically present in the jurisdiction does not violate due process).

88   Murphy E-mail, supra note 65.

89   See supra notes 13 & 14. Trimbach claims she survived the gun shot and fall. Trimbach, supra note 36, at 2.

90   The trust land status of Amiotte's ranch reflects how hard the Pine Ridge Reservation was hit by the General Allotment (Dawes) Act, ch. 119, 24 Stat. 388 (1887) (codified as amended at 25 U.S.C. § 331), repudiated by the Indian Reorganization Act, ch. 576, 48 Stat. 984 (1934) (codified as amended at 25 U.S.C. §§ 461-77). See Trimbach, supra note 36, at 52-53.

91   Fed. R. Civ. P. 12(b)(1). See supra note 82.

92   18 U.S.C. § 1151(c); Cf. S.D. Codified Laws § 31-4-176 (defining state highway 73).

93   See supra notes 28 and 90.

94   18 U.S.C. § 1151(c); see supra note 90.

95   Ambiotte Testimony, see supra note 28.

96   Merrick Testimony, id. Did she fall after being shot, or was her body thrown down the cliff?

97   Looking Cloud II, 419 F.2d at 790; Graham III, 815 N.W.2d at 296.

98   *United States v. Thirion*, 813 F.2d 146, 151 (8th Cir. 1987) (holding that that an extradited defendant can only be charged for offenses he was extradited for, unless the asylum country consents).

99   Graham III, 815 N.W.2d at 298-300.

100   Affidavit of Chief Jerry Kapilano (Mar. 2, 2005), in Ghost Rider Roads 257, see supra note 8.

101   U.S. Const. Art. IV, § 2, cl. 2.

102   18 U.S.C. § 3182.

103   See the "bad men" clauses of the Navajo Treaty art. 1, July 25, 1868, 15 Stat. 667, 1868 WL 24281; and Navajo Nation Code tit. 7, § 607, available at http://www.navajocourts.org /Tit7.htm.

104   Hon. Kerstin G. LeMaire & Mark D. Tallan, Issues Involving Extradition and Their Impact on Tribal Sovereignty, 76 U. Det. Mercy L. Rev. 803, 820 (Spring 1999).

105   413 F.2d 683 (9th Cir. 1969), cert. denied, 396 U.S. 1003 (1970) (affirming extradition language in the Navajo Treaty of 1868 to prove states cannot arrest Indians on Indian Territory).

106   462 N.W.2d 463 (S.D. 1990).

107   Id. at 464-465. Art. III of the Jay Treaty (1794) and Treaty of Ghent, 8 Stat. 218 (1814), have long been raised to prove Indians may freely pass the border between Canada and the United States, put into law by The Immigration and Nationality Act of 1952, § 289, and codified by 8 U.S.C. § 1359.

108   Def. Graham's Mem. in Supp. Of Mot. To Dismiss Indictment at 2-8, Graham I (D.S.D. Sep. 23, 2008), available at 2008 WL 4360469.

109   Rios's house in Rapid City was not on Indian Territory; see supra, note 47.

110   *United States v. Rogers*, 45 U.S. 567 (1846) (holding that adopted into the Cherokee is still white).

111   Clinton, supra note 66, at 513-14, n. 48.

112   Id.

113   Indian Entities Recognized and Eligible to Receive Services From the Bureau of Indian Affairs, 77 Fed. Reg. 47868 (Aug. 10, 2012), available at http://www.bia.gov/cs/groups /public/documents/text/idc002652.pdf.

114   Some sources erroneously state his ethnicity as Tsimshian, which might have been an easy analysis as the United States recognizes this ethic group as the predominant part of the Metlakatla Indian Community which occupies the Annette Island Reservation in Alaska.

115   In Alaska, Athabaskan bloodlines could include eight recognized villages of the Ahtna corporation and others in Cook Inlet. Even Hupa, Navajo, and Apache Tribes are Athabaskan.

116   Treaty of Watertown, Jul. 19, 1776, available at http://historicalsocietyofwatertownma. org/HSW/HSWdocs/treatyofwatertown.pdf.

117   In re Wanomi P., 216 Cal.App.3d 156 (Cal.App. 2d Dist. 1989).

118   See supra note 115.

119   Charles F. Wilkinson & John M. Volkman, Judicial Review of Indian Treaty Abrogation: "As Long as Water Flows or Grass Grows upon the Earth"—How Long is That?, 63 *Cal. L. Rev.* 601, 608-19 (1975).

120   See supra note 96. Cf. *United States v. Stymiest*, 581 F.3d 759, 763-64 (8th Cir. 2009) (reciting the Rogers test, but also giving five more factors for the second prong which are optional in the 8th Circuit).

121   See supra note 75.

122   See three popular documentary and news films cited infra notes 126, 132, and 136.

123   Looking Cloud I, see supra note 11 (citing the testimony of Ka-Mook "Darlene" Nichols, and that she overheard Peltier brag, "[Williams] was begging for his life, but I shot him anyway."

124   The now largely forgotten notion that Aquash was raped before she was killed has always been nonetheless a factor in this martyrdom. See supra note 62.

125   Aside from celebrities supporting clemency for Peltier, Senators Daniel Inouye and

James Abourezk were ardently campaigning for Peltier in the 1990s.

126		*American Justice: Murder on the Reservation* (A&E television broadcast Oct. 17, 2000).

127		Trimbach, supra note 36.

128		Id. at 3.

129		Id.at 427-28.

130		For a similar case to Peltier's involving the Texas Rangers, see generally Ott v. State, 627 S.W.2d 218 (Tex. Ct. App. 1981).

131		Trimbach, supra note 36.

132		*Incident at Oglala* (Miramax 1992).

133		As romanticized in the film *Mississippi Burning* (Orion 1988).

134		Oliver North is among those endorsing Trimbach's book; Trimbach, supra note 36, at back cover.

135		Some of the more memorable name-calling Trimbach employs are in id., at 484 ("feel-good do-nothings"); at 455 ("lonely fantasist"); at 469 ("reservation wise-guy"); and at 495 ("linguini-spined jurists").

136		Id., at 601 n. 76; see *Incident at Oglala*, supra note 132 and 60 Minutes: The Last Sioux Brave? (CBS television broadcast Sep. 22, 1991).

137		See *Incident at Oglala*, supra note 132 (quoting Poor Bear as saying "And they showed me pictures of her hands—just her hands. And then they told me, 'well, if you don't cooperate, it's going to be worse with you.' He said, 'we'll put you through a meat grinder, where no one will ever know.'").

138		*60 Minutes*, supra note 136.

139		*American Justice*, supra note 126.

140		Trudell admits AIM members all had criminal records. Incident at Oglala, supra note 132.

141		Id.

142		An anti-AIM website reminds its readers of the mysterious death of a Black Panther member participating in the demonstration, Ray Robinson, Jr. See supra note 10.

143		*Incident at Oglala*, supra note 132.

144		Id. (quoting Senator James Abourezk saying "Well it sort of fizzled out as everyone was just tired of it and I think the Indians were as tired of it as the Government was. They finally just agreed to a 'let's all give up at the same time. We'll put you on trial for certain things,' that's how it ended.")

145		This allowed FBI agents to deny that COINTELPRO tactics were ever used on AIM. See Trimbach, supra note 36.

146		Id. at 276-78.

147		Id. At 183.

148		*American Justice*, supra note 126.

149		Wood Testimony, supra note 45.

150		Trimbach, supra note 36, at 356-57.

151		Billie Pierre, *US Renews War on American Indians: The Anna Mae Pictou-Aquash Story* (Jan./Feb. 2006), https://mgouldhawke.wordpress.com/us-renews-war-on-the-american-indian-movementthe-anna-mae-pictou-aquash-story/ (last visited Aug. 1, 2022).

152		Trudell also hints at some sort of larger plan with the cowboy boot theft used only as a cover story. Incident at Oglala, supra note 132.

153		Trimbach's attempt to depict Eagle's crime as one more of torture then theft still fails to explain why this received so much attention. See Trimbach, supra note 36, at 412.

154		*60 Minutes*, supra note 136.

155		Mathiessen, supra note 4, at 175-76.

156		Id. at 580.

157		*60 Minutes*, supra note 136.

158   *Incident at Oglala*, supra note 132.

159   Id. and 60 Minutes, supra note 136.

160   See Jane Kinney, Out of Hand: An Interview with Leonard Peltier, *Plazm* (Nov. 16, 2015), available at https://magazine.plazm.com/out-of-hand-e17403530ed9.

161   *American Justice*, supra note 126.

162   Kinney, supra note 160.

163   Trimbach, supra note 36, at 495.

164   Id.; quoting Chris Summers, Native American Prisoner to Fight On, BBC News Online, April 24, 2004, http://news.bbc.co.uk/2/hi/americas/3654785.stm (last accessed Aug. 1, 2022).

165   See supra note 43.

166   See infra note 224.

167   See Some Indians: Dennis Banks and Anna Mae Aquash, http://www.dancingbadger.com/dennisb03.html (last visited Aug. 1, 2022).

168   See supra note 51.

169   Supra notes 11 and 123.

170   Trimbach, supra note 36, at 453-55.

171   Supra notes 11 and 123. Also conveniently inserted into the trial is Looking Cloud conveniently nodding his head when handing Graham the gun. United States v. Looking Cloud, supra note 11, at 790.

172   *News From Indian County* Archives, https://www.wortfm.org/tag/news-from-indian-county/ (last visited Aug. 1, 2022).

173   See infra note 214.

174   See Gregg Wager, Churchill's Finest Hour?, *Village Voice* (Mar. 1, 2005), available at http://www.villagevoice.com/2005-03-01/specials/letters/full/ .

175   Trimbach, supra note 36, at 471; quoting Russell Means, Where White Men Fear to Tread (1996), at 362.

176   *Incident at Oglala*, supra note 132.

177   *American Justice*, supra note 126.

178   Id.

179   Richard Goldstein, Bill Jankow, a Four-Term Governor of South Dakota, Dies at 72, *New York Times* (Jan. 12, 2012), available at http://www.nytimes.com/2012/01/13/us/bill-janklow-a-four-term-governor-of-south-dakota-dies-at-72.html?_r=0 .

180   Matthiessen, supra note 4, at 594-96.

181   See Revenge Served Cold, available at http://dancingbadger.com/jancita_eagle_deer.htm .

182   See supra note 1.

183   Trimbach, supra note 36, at 334-35.

184   Id.

185   Id.

186   Matthiessen, supra note 4, at 211.

187   Trimbach, supra note 36, at 327.

188   Matthiessen, supra note 4, at 205.

189   Id.

190   Id. at 155; see also id., xvii (showing a map of the Jumping Bull Compound).

191   Id. at 204.

192   Id. at 205.

193   Id. at 155.

194   Id.

195   *American Justice*, supra note 126.

196 Matthiessen, supra note 4, at 156.

197 *Incident at Oglala*, supra note 132.

198 Trimbach, supra note 36, at 423.

199 Id. at 399.

200 Id.

201 Matthiessen, supra note 4, at 155; quoted in Trimbach, supra note 36, 399.

202 Matthiessen, supra note 4, at 204-05.

203 Id.

204 *Incident at Oglala*, supra note 132.

205 Id.

206 Id.

207 Id.

208 *United States v. Peltier*, 800 F.2d 772, 772-73 (8th Cir. 1986).

209 See *United States v. Bagley*, 473 U.S. 667 (1985).

210 *Incident at Oglala*, supra note 132.

211 Id.

212 See the film *Thunderheart* (TriStar Pictures 1992).

213 This detail appears to be especially contrived by the FBI as a way to convict Bill Means for something.

214 See supra note 10; and Oneida Eye, http://oneidaeye.com/2013/09/10/paul-de-mains-comments-on-leonard-peltier-tribunal/ (last visited Aug. 1, 2022).

215 Matthiessen, supra note 4, at 146 (using actually the word "bullshitted" to describe the mood at this meeting).

216 Id.

217 Letter in Claypoole, supra note 8, at 91-93.

218 Interview between Claypoole and Graham, Id. at 506.

219 815 N.W.2d at 306.

220 Jennifer Wicke, *Postmodern Identity and the Legal Subject*, 62 U. Colo. L. Rev. 455, 457 (1991). This follows the definition of "postmodernism" as it was originally applied to music. See Gregg Wager, Post-Modern Music: "Condominium of Babel." *L.A. Times* (13 Feb. 1988) part VI: 5+.

221 See Francis J. Mootz, III, *Is the Rule of Law Possible in a Postmodern World?*, 68 Wash. L. Rev. 249 (1993).

222 See supra, note 1. Antoinette Nora Claypoole, *Who Would Unbraid Her Hair: The Legend of Annie Mae* xv-xviii (Anam Cara Press, 1999) (listing 61 of the casualties).

223 See Mootz, supra note 221.

224 Barbara Ann Atwood, Flashpoints Under the Indian Child Welfare Act: Toward a new Understanding of State Court Resistance, 51 Emory L.J. 587 (2002); and Sandra C. Ruffin, Postmodernism, Spirit Healing, and the Proposed Amendments to the Indian Child Welfare Act, 30 McGeorge L. Rev. 1221 (1999).

225 417 U.S. 535 (1974) (holding that hiring preference for an "Indian" was a political, not racial, classification); see supra note 79.

226 Rebecca Tsosie, American Indians and the Politics of Recognition: Soifer on Law, Pluralism, and Group Identity, 22 *Law & Soc. Inquiry* 359, 361 (1997) (taking exception to Aviam Soifer's proposed constitutional right of association, suggesting that the law should reflect that there are different reasons for preserving different identities).

227 Telephone Interview with Janis Schmidt Interview (Mar. 24, 5:30 PM).

228 Wood Testimony, supra note 45.

229 Janis Schmidt, whose eviction saga off of the Pine Ridge Indian Reservation because of her Aquash investigation is related in the case *Schmidt v. Bodin*, 2007 WL 2362583 (S.D. Dist.Ct. Aug. 15, 2007) (Civ. No. 06-5034), suggests that "John Boy Patton" is not a nickname for John Graham,

but a second person who actually was a cousin of Clarke and who actually killed Aquash. Schmidt Interview, supra note 210. Bachrach believes the courts got the detail of the event correct, but failed by not indicting Clarke or any of the ultimate decision-makers in both AIM and FBI (see supra note 28); Antoinette Nora Claypoole emphasizes FBI reports of sighting of Aquash driving a blue Mustang convertible in Oklahoma early in 1976. Special Agent David F. Price, FBI, United States Memorandum to SAC, Minneapolis (Feb. 18, 1976), in Ghost Rider Roads 466, see supra note 8.

230   Charles Michael Ray, S.D. Tribe Poised to Take Back Part of Badlands, NPR (May 25, 2012).

231   Radke-Uhlmann , supra note 25.

232   Cf. generally Francis J. Mootz, III, *Law and Philosophy, Philosophy and Law*, 26 U. Tol. L. Rev. 127 (1994).

233   See infra note 236.

234   Francis Lieber, *Legal and Political Hermeneutics, or Principles of Interpretation and Construction in Law and Politics, with Remarks on Precedents and Authorities* (Roy M. Mersky & J. Myron Jacobstein eds., Hein & Co., photo. reprint 1970) (1839).

235   *Mayor of New York v. Lord,* 18 Wend. 126, 131 (N.Y. Sup. Ct. 1837) (mentioning that legal hermeneutics provides "fixed principles of interpretation" and ascertains " 'the meaning and intent of the lawgiver.' "). This and other early cases that mentioned legal hermeneutics were written by Reuben H. Walworth, who served as Chancellor of New York from 1828 to 1847.

236   Lieber, supra note 234, at 143-44. (listing 16 general rules of construction); and at 167-72 (listing 18 rules of construction for statutes and contracts); at 177-90 (listing 11 rules of Constitutional construction).

237   *Donaldson v. Wood & Wood,* 22 Wend. 395, 397 (N.Y. 1839); *McCluskey v. Cromwell,* 11 N.Y. 593, 603 (N.Y. 1854); *Molony v. Dows,* 8 Abb. Pr. 316, 331 (N.Y. Ct. C.P. 1859); *Moore v. Wood,* 19 How. Pr. 405, 406-07 (N.Y. Gen. Term 1860); *McColl v. Sun Mut. Ins. Co.,* 44 How. Pr. 452, 454-55 (N.Y. 1872); *O'Brien v. Mechanics' and Traders' Fire Ins. Co.,* 44 How. Pr. 452, 454-55 (N.Y. Gen. Term 1872); *Wayne Cnty. Sav. Bank v. Low,* 6 Abb. N. Cas. 76, 88 (N.Y. 1878); *Gabel v. Williams,* 80 N.Y.S. 489, 495 (N.Y. Oneida Cnty. Ct. 1902); *People ex rel. Folk v. McNulty,* 56 A.D. 82, 97 (N.Y. App. Div. 1939); *Lasro Corp. v. Kree Inst. of Electrolysis, Inc.,* 215 N.Y.S.2d 125, 128 (N.Y. N.Y.C. Mun. Ct. 1961); *Uniformed Firefighters Ass'n Local 94 v Beekman,* 420 N.E.2d 938, 943 (N.Y. 1981); and *People v. Doe,* 642 N.Y.S.2d 996, 998 (N.Y. Nassau Cnty. Ct. 1996).

238   Most notably cases from before World War II coming out of state courts in Tennessee, Louisiana, Mississippi, and Georgia.

239   *Redman v. Barger,* 24 S.W. 177, 178 (Mo. 1893); *Cornwell v. Wulff,* 50 S.W. 439, 448 (Mo. 1898); *Cross v. Hock,* 50 S.W. 786, 788 (Mo. 1899); *State ex rel. Major v. Ryan,* 133 S.W. 8, 12 (Mo. 1910); and *Gulley v. Waggoner,* 164 S.W. 557, 560 (Mo. 1914).

240   *People v. Coffey,* 199 P. 901, 905 (Cal. 1911); *People v. Stanley,* 269 P. 465, 467 (Cal. Dist. Ct. App. 1928); and *People v. Wallin,* 188 P. 764, 65 (Cal. Dist. Ct. App. 1948).

241   See Scalia, supra notes 14 and 22.

242   See *Continental Can Co., Inc. v. Chi. Truck Drivers, Helpers and Warehouse Workers Union* (Indep.) Pension Fund, 916 F.2d 1154, 1157 (7th Cir. 1990); and *Mercado v. Ahmed,* 756 F.Supp. 1097, 1099 n. 2 (N.D. Ill. 1991).

243   *Stupak-Thrall v. United States,* 89 F.3d 1269 (6th Cir. 1996).

244   The Michigan Wilderness Act, Pub. L. No. 100-184, 101 Stat. 1274 (Dec. 8, 1987).

245   Crooked Lake in Gogebic County, a small, remote body of water in Ottawa national Forest, where question is raised if such craft as sail boats and house boats ever were present there in the first place. The challenge to the regulations dealt more with a hypothetical situation, if Gogebic County dwellers ever wanted to use sail boats and house boats there. Stupak-Thrall, 89 F.3d at 1271.

246   Id. at 1272.

247   Anthony D'Amato, *Aspects of Deconstruction: The "Easy Case" of the Under-Aged President,* 84 Nw. U. L. Rev. 250 (1989) (covering Judge Easterbrook's commentary about possible flexibility in the law, since better times allow an earlier age for puberty and a longer life expectancy).

248   Francis J. Mootz, III, *The Ontological Basis of Legal Hermeneutics: A Proposed Model of Inquiry Based on the Work of Gadamer, Habermas, and Ricoeur,* 68 B.U. L. Rev. 523 (1988).

249   See supra notes 234 and 236.

250   Gadamer, supra note 15, at 434.

251   Id. at 511; Martin Heidegger, *Sein und Zeit* (17th ed. 1993) (1927).

252   René Descartes, *Discours de la méthod* (1637).

253   Immanuel Kant, *Critik der Urteilskraft* [Critique of the Power of Judgment] (Wilhelm Weischedel ed., 1974) (1790).

254   Gadamer, supra note 15, at 297.

255   See generally Klaus W. Hempfer, Überlegungen zur möglichen Rationalität(sform), supra note 25, at 267-68.

256   See Jürgen Habermas, Erläuterungen zur Diskursethik 81-92 (1991).

257   See Arbogast Schmitt, Phronesis—"eine andere Art des Erkennens", supra note 25, at 63.

258   See also Heidegger, supra note 251, at 96.

259   Gadamer, supra note 15, at 250.

260   Heidegger famously divides this fore-structure into three forms which are difficult to translate (Vorhabe, Vorsicht, Vorgriff); see Heidegger, supra note 251, at 150.

261   Aristotle, supra note 13, at 398.1-10.

262   See Schmitt, supra notes 25 and 257, at 55.

263   Heidegger, supra note 251, at 41-45.

264   Id., at 17-19.

265   Id., at 142-148 (discussing these aspects under the title "§ 31. Das Da-sein als Verstehen").

266   Id., at 56.

267   Augustine, *Confessions* 58 (Frank J. Sheed trans., 1993) (stating that "facticia est anima").

268   Heidegger, supra note 251, at 148.

269   Josh Michael Hayes, Dasein: Heidegger's Earliest Interpretation of Aristotle's "De Anima", 61.2 Rev. Metaphysics 266-68 (2007).

270   See Jürgen Habermas, Urbanisierung der Heideggerschen Provinz: Laudatio an Hans-Georg Gadamer, Das Erbe Hegels (1979).

271   See Gianni Vattimo, *The End of Modernity, Nihilism and Hermeneutics in Post-Modern Culture* (Jon R. Snyder trans., 1988).

272   Habermas 1979, supra note 270, at 13.

273   See Hayes, supra note 269, at 263-64.

274   Heidegger, supra note 251, at 148-53 (discussing these aspects under the title "§ 32. Verstehen und Auslegung").

275   Id., at 7.

276   Id., at 153.

277   Id.

278   Gadamer, supra note 15, at 251.

279   Heidegger, supra note 251, at 118.

280   Id., at 133 note "a."

281   See infra note 284.

282   See generally supra note 25.

283   Id.

284   See generally Louis Menand, *The Metaphysical Club: A Story of Ideas in America* 207 (2001) (mentioning the positivism of Chauncey Wright (1830-1875) as a conscious and "absolute separation" between fact and values, holding the latter depreciatingly to be a purely metaphysical area and not to be ever confused with science).

285   See Gyburg Radke-Uhlmann, Ist die Vernunft trivial? Studien zum Wandel der wissenschaften vom menschlichen Geist, supra note 25, at 210.

286   See generally Friedrich Schleiermacher, Hermeneutick und Kritik (Suhrkamp 1977).

287   As opposed to the traditional three parts of Catholicism: allegorical, moral, and anagogical.

288   See Heidegger, supra note 251, at 397-404 (discussing these aspects under the title "§ 77. Der Zusammenhang der vorstehenden Exposition des problems der Geschichtlichkeit mit den forschungen W. Diltheys und den Ideen des Grafen Yorck").

289   Justice Anthony Kennedy in a lecture at McGeorge Law School Sep. 4, 2012.

290   See Paul Ricœur, *The Rule of Metaphor* 151 (Robert Czerny trans., 1977).

291   Mao-Tse Tung, *Quotations from Chairman Mao-Tse Tung* (1964).

292   Scalia, supra note 14, at 38.

293   See generally supra note 284.

294   Aside from Aristotle, who originally employed the Greek word ἑρμηνεύω, early and extensively developed systems for theological interpretation include St. Augustine (sensus literalis, sensus allegoricus sensus tropologicus, and sensus anagogicus); St. Thomas Aquinas (per modum cognitionis v. per modum inclinationis); and Martin Luther (scriptura sacra sui ipsius interpres).

295   The Prussian Code, introduction, 46, even included a law against interpreting the laws. See Lieber, supra note 234, at 126-27.

296   See supra note 253.

297   Immanuel Kant, *Critik der reinen Vernunft* [Critique of Pure Reason] 217 (Ingeborg Heidemann ed., 1966) (1787); quoted in Heidegger, supra note 251, 23.

298   Id.

299   See generally Douglas Hofstadter, *Gödel, Escher, and Bach: an Eternal Golden Braid* (1979).

300   See generally Schleiermacher, supra note 286.

301   Lieber, supra note 234, at 94f.

302   Id.

303   *Church of the Holy Trinity v. United States*, 143 U.S. 457 (1892); see Scalia, supra note 14, at 18-23.

304   Id.at 22.

305   For a comprehensive overview of the various current usages of termini derived from "originalism," such as parsing a distinction between "original meaning" and "original intent," see Keith E. Whittington, Originalism: A Critical Introduction, 82 Fordham L. Rev. 375, 379-382 (2013).

306   See Friedo Ricken, Die Vernunftform des religiösen Glaubens und der Theologie, supra note 25, at 169; especially noteworthy is Ricken's description of how Aristotle warned against the youthful propensity to confine the interpretation of laws only to the "dead letters of a law book." Id., at 172; see also John Henry Newman, An Essay in Aid of a Grammar of Assent 276 (1874); and Thomas Aquinas, *Summa Totius Theologiæ* 56 (Venice, 1778) (1274).

307   Scalia, supra note 14, at 17.

308   Id.at 3.

309   Id. at 8.

310   Id. at 15; see Jabiz Gridley Sutherland, *Statutes and Statutory Construction* (1891).

311   At least some philosophers have proposed mixing natural sciences with more conventional philosophy, without resorting to the extremes of naturalism or logical positivism. See W.V. Quine, Ontological Relativity and Other Essays 69-90 (1969).

312   See Scalia, supra note 14, at 14.

313   See generally supra notes 284 and 311.

314   See Scalia, supra note 14, at 38.

315   Id.

316   Id. at 17-18.

317   Id.

318   Harmelin v. Michigan, 501 U.S. 957, 966-68 (1991).

319   In comparison, the California Constitution only requires the banned punishment to be "cruel or unusual." Cal. Const. art. I, § 17; this made it much easier to ban the death penalty in California. People v. Anderson, 493 P.2d 880 (Cal. 1972), repealed by Cal. "Proposition 17" (1972).

320   Solem v. Helm, 463 U.S. 277, 290-902 (1983).

321   Anthony F. Granucci, "Nor Cruel and Unusual Punishments Inflicted:" The Original Menaing, 57 Calif. L. Rev. 839 (1969).

322   Id., at 840-41 n. 8.

323   See Titus Oates, *To the Right Honorable Lords Spiritual and Temporal the Humble Petition of titus oates*, D.D. 1 (1689), in 10 Cobbett's Complete Collection of State Trials col. 1325 (T. Howell ed., 1811), also in Granucci, supra note 80, at 858 n. 90-91; this petition is also cited in the minority opinion by Justice Edward Douglass White (written only seven months before he was appointed Chief Justice) of Weems v. United States, 217 U.S. 349, 390-92 (1910).

324   "Boilerplate" is Granucci's own word; Granucci, supra note 321, at 840.

325   Harmelin, 501 U.S. at 967.

326   Id. (probably confusing the "English Bill of Rights" with the "Virginia Declaration of Rights").

327   Granucci, supra note 321, 854.

328   Id.

329   In all fairness to Scalia, Granucci is also probably too generous in his broad assessments by "most historians" of the ultimate source of "cruel and unusual." Id., at 853.

330   See supra, notes 301 and 302.

331   Harmelin, 501 U.S. at 968.

332   Id.

333   Id.

334   Granucci, supra note 321, at 858.

335   See supra, note 329.

336   The word "unique" is introduced into the opinion by quoting from *Furman v. Georgia*, 408 U.S. 238, 306 (1972).

337   Harmelin, 501 U.S. at 995.

338   Id., at 996.

339   Id.

340   Id.

341   Leviticus 24:17-21.

342   *District of Columbia v. Heller*, 554 U.S. 570 (2008).

343   See supra note 290.

344   See Robert Louis Stevenson, *Kidnapped* (1886).

345   See supra note 306.

346   Jürgen Habermas, *Zur Logik der Sozialwissenschaften* 284-85 (Suhrkamp 1967).

347   *See generally* Purushottama Bilimoria, Towards a Creative hermeneutic of Susipicion: Recovering Ricoeur's Intervention in the Gadamer-Habermas Debate, World Philosophy Conference Proceedings (1999), available at http://www.bu.edu/wcp/Papers/Cont/ContBili.htm .

348   Id.

349   Paul Ricœur, Le conflit des interprétations (1969).

350   See generally Friedrich Nietzsche, Nietzsche Contra Wagner (1895).

351   See The Marquis de Sade, *Florville and Courval, or The Works of Fate, The* 120 Days of *Sodom and Other Writings* 133-80 (Austryn Wainhouse and Richard Seaver trans., 1966).

352   Friedrich Nietzsche, *Menschliches Allzumenschliches* 1 (1878).

353   See Bilimoria, supra note 347.

354   Id.

355 Heidegger, supra note 251, 71.

356 Gadamer, supra note 15, 434ff.

357 Id., at 123ff.

358 Bertolt Brecht, *On Chinese Acting*, 6.1 Tulane Drama R. 130-36 (trans, Eric Bentley, 1961).

359 Karl Marx, Ökonomisches-Philosophische Manuskripte 156 (1970).

360 Gadamer, supra note 15, at 156f.

361 Brecht, supra note 358.

362 Habermas 1967, supra note 346, 281.

363 Id.

364 See Michel Foucault, Foucault Live 30 (1989).

365 See Wager, supra note 220.

366 Id.

367 Jean-François Lyotard, *La Condition postmoderne* (1979); and *The Postmodern Condition* (G. Bennington & B. Massumi trs., 1984).

368 See generally Francis Fukuyama, *The End of History and the Last Man* (1992).

369 See Mootz, supra note 221.

370 Barbara Ann Atwood and Ruffin, supra note 224.

371 Jennifer Wicke, *Postmodern Identity and the Legal Subject*, 62 U. Colo. L. Rev. 455, 457 (1991).

372 See Lyotard 1984, supra note 367.

373 Id.

374 Id.at 30-35.

375 Id.at 11.

376 Id., quoting generally Talcott Parsons, *The Social System* (1967) and *Sociological Thinking and Modern Society* (1967).

377 Fredric Jameson, Foreword, in Lyotard 1979, supra note 367, at xix.

378 Id. at xxiv.

379 See Lyotard 1984, supra note 367 at 34.

380 Jameson, supra note 377, at xii.

381 Ihab Hassan, *The Dismemberment of Orpheus* 23 (1971).

382 See generally Michel Foucault, *The Archeology of Knowledge* (1972); and same, Discipline and Punish (1979).

383 See generally Gilles Deleuze and Félix Guattari, Anti-Oedipus (1983).

384 Jean Baudrillard, *Forget Foucault* 67-68 (1987).

385 Jameson, supra note 377.

386 See generally Ernesto Laclau and Chantal Mouffe, *Hegemony and Social Strategist* (1985)

387 See generally Steven Best and Douglas Kellner, *Postmodern Theory* 159 (1991).

388 See the 70-page "John Galt Speech" toward the end of Ayn Rand, *Atlas Shrugged* 1000-70 (1957).

389 See supra note 368.

390 Gianni Vattimo, Hermeneutic Communism (2011). The so-called "Pink Tide" consists primarily of Hugo Chávez in Venezuela, Daniel Ortega in Nicaragua, Rafael Correa in Ecuador, and Evo Morales in Bolivia.

391 Natalie Obiko Pearson, Chavez: Assassination Attempt Foiled, *Washington Post* (Sep. 30, 2006), available at http://www.washingtonpost.com/wp-dyn/content/article/2006/09/30/AR2006093001317.html .

392 See generally Dilip Hiro, *Apocalyptic Realm* 205-10 (2012).

393 See Jean-Jacque Nattiez, *Music and Discourse: Toward a Semiology of Music* (Carolyn Abbate trs., 1990).

394   Hayden White, *The Value of Narrativity in the Representation of Reality*, Critical Inquiry 7.1, 5 (Autumn 1980).

395   Id. at 5-6.

396   Gérard Genette, *Boundaries of Narrative*, New Literary History 8.1, 11 (Autumn 1976) (quoted in White, supra note 377, at 7).

397   Jean-François Lyotard and Jean-Loup Thébaud, *Just Gaming 90* (trans. Wlad Godzich, 1985); quoted in Best and Kellner, supra note 387, at 159.

398   Jean-François Lyotard, The Differend (trans. Georges Van Den Abbeele, 1988).

399   Wovon man nicht sprechen kann, darüber muss man schweigen (whatever one cannot talk about, one must shut up about). Ludwig Wittgenstein, Logische-Philosophische Abhandlung 75 (1921).

400   Robert Cover, *The Supreme Court, 1982 Term*—Foreword: Nomos and Narrative, 97 Harv. L. Rev. 4 (1983), reprinted in Martha Minow, Michael Ryan, and Austin Sarat, eds., Narrative, Violence, and the Law 95 (1995).

401   Id. at 117.

402   Id.

403   Ezra 1:1-5.

404   What Justice Anthony Kennedy referred to as "splitting the jurisdiction atom" Justice in a lecture at McGeorge Law School Sep. 4, 2012.

405   See generally Jürgen Habermas, Legitimationsprobleme im Spätkapitalismus (1973).

406   See generally Jürgen Habermas, Faktizität und Geltung (1992), published in English as Between Facts and Norms (William Rehg trans., 1996).

407   See generally Jürgen Habermas, Theorie des kommunikatives Handelns (1981).

408   Best and Kellner, supra note 387, at 240.

409   See generally Bilimoria, supra note 353.

410   See generally John Hospers, *Libertarianism: A Political Philosophy for Tomorrow* (2013) (1971).

411   Lyotard 1984, supra note 367, at 79.

412   Best and Kellner, supra note 387, at 255 n. 9.

413   Id.

414   Lyotard 1984, supra note 367, 73.

415   Lyotard et al. 1984, supra note 397.

416   See generally Chantal Mouffe, *The Democratic Paradox* (2000).

417   See generally Habermas 1973, supra note 405.

418   See generally Habermas 1992, supra note 406.

419   See generally supra notes 405 and 406.

420   Habermas 1992, supra note 406, at 112-18 (German), and at 84-89 (English).

421   Id.at 115-16 (German) and at 88 (English).

422   Id. at 84 (English) and 5 (German)

423   Id.

424   Id. At 107 (English) and 138 (German).

425   Id.; cf. supra notes 420 and 421 (demonstrating why the translator perhaps chose the word "law" as opposed to "right," since Habermas wanted to reserve "human rights" to the moral side of the equation, and law to the "popular sovereignty" side, although the confusion in translation also illustrates why it is so difficult to pin down these concepts in terms of the simply left/right political dichotomy in both American and Germany).

426   In making this postulate, it is assumed Habermas is using the Roman letter "D" to stand of "discourse." Id. (D: Gültig sind genau die Handlungsnormen, denen alle möglicherweise Betroffenen als Teilnehmer an rationalen Diskursen zustimmen könnten.)

427   See generally Hospers, supra note 410.

428   Habermas 1992, supra note 406, at 125 (German) (Selbstbestimmung), and at 95 (English).

429   Id. (Selbstverwirklichung).

430   Id. at 99 (English) and at 128-29 (German) (Diese Ideen von Selbstbestimmung und Selbstverwirklichung harmonieren freilich nicht ohne wieteres miteinander. Deshalb hat auch das Vernunftrecht auf did modernen Gerechtigkeitsideen und Lebensideale mit jeweils anders akzentuierten Antworten reagiert.)

431   See generally Best and Kellner, supra note 387, at 246-55.

432   See H.L.A. Hart, *The Concept of Law* 107 (1961) quoted in Habermas, supra note 407, at 248 n. 12 (German), and at 202 n. 12 (English) (showing that courts adapt that rule of recognition between two opposing parties who must recognize the other as facticity).

433   Best and Kellner, supra note 387, at 246.

434   These three categories of discourse stem generally from Kant's trilogy: Kritik der reinen Vernunft, supra note 297, Kritik der praktischen Vernunft (1788), and Kritik der Urteilskraft, supra note 253.

435   Habermas 1992, supra note 406, at 141 (German) (Das diskurstheoretisch begriffene Moralprinzip überschreitet schon die historisch zufälligen und je nach Sozialstruktur anders verlaufenden Grenzen zwischen privaten und öffentlichen Lebensbereich;...) and at 109 (English).

436   Lyotard 1988, supra note 398, at 64.

437   Best and Kellner, supra note 387, at 249.

438   Id. at 250 ("In a sense the debate between Lyotard and Habermas is a squabble amongst neo-Kantians, for both have come to share a certain neo-Kantian terrain.").

439   Lyotard 1988, supra note 398, at 136.

440   Best and Kellner, supra note 387, at 244.

441   See Billamoria, supra note 347.

442   Atwood, supra note 224, at 598.

443   Ruffin, supra note 224, at 1222.

444   *Adoptive Couple v. Baby Girl*, 133 S.Ct. 2552 (2013).

445   See Meg Kennard, Melanie Capobianco, Adoptive Mother of "Baby Girl"Veronica: "It's About Her," Huffington Post (Aug. 8, 2013), available at http://www.huffingtonpost.com/2013/08/08/matt-and-melanie-capobianco-veronica-adoption-case_n_3726145.html .

446   For a discussion of various blood quanta requirements for the Federally recognized tribes that the ICWA is to apply to, see Atwood, supra note 224, at 607 note 83.

447   In the 5-4 decision, J. Sotomayor wrote the dissent joined by J. Kagen and J. Ginsberg. J. Scalia wrote a separate dissent.

448   *Adoptive Couple*, supra note 444 at 2562.

449   Id. at 2560.

450   d. at 2571-72.

451   Id. at 2584, citing *United States v. Antelope*, 430 U.S. 641 (1977) (comparing the Federal Major Crimes Act and Idaho Criminal Code and ruling that the Equal Protection Clause did not apply based on the evenhandedness of the Federal law, even though plenary power granted to Congress and historical decisions of the past allow for racial classifications for American Indians) and Morton v. Mancari, 417 U.S. 535 (1974) (holding that the BIA may preferentially hire American Indians over other racial classifications).

452   *Adoptive Couple*, supra note 444, at 2565; cf. supra note 451.

453   "Reclaiming History" is not only the title of the second part of Trimbach, supra note 21, at 347, but also of a famous Kennedy book by a famous Los Angeles prosecutor. See Vincent Bugliosi, *Reclaiming History: The Assassination of John F. Kennedy* (2007).

454   Trimbach even takes on the myths about J. Edgar Hoover, depicting him as an American legend with few faults. Trimbach, supra note 36, at 34-48.

455   Id. at vii-ix. See supra note 36.

456   See Mark Twain, *The Adventures of Tom Sawyer* (1876).

457   See L. Frank Baum, *The Wizard of Oz* (1900).

458   See The Keith Olbermann Forum (Feb. 28, 2011, 11:28 P.M.) available at http://keitholbermann.org/forum/viewtopic.php?f=70&t=26350 .

459   See Albert Ehrenzweig, *The Transient Rule of Personal Jurisdiction: The "Power" of Myth and Forum Conviens*, 65 Yale L. J. 289, 296 (Jan. 1956).

460   See Hospers, supra note 410.

461   See Hassan, supra note 381.

462   See Fukuyama, supra note 368.

463   See Wager 1991, supra note 365.

464   Cf. Hassan, supra note 381, at 14-17 (claiming John Cage was actually a postmodern composer).

465   See Lyotard 1984, supra note 367.

466   Ron Paul, End the Fed (2009).

467   Thomas Meehan (book), *Annie* (1977).

Index